THE EGYPTIAN
BOOK OF THE
DEAD

THE EGYPTIAN BOOK OF THE DEAD

TRANSLATED BY E.A. WALLIS BUDGE

SIRIUS

CONTENTS

SIRIUS

This edition published in 2025 by Sirius Publishing, a division of
Arcturus Publishing Limited,
26/27 Bickels Yard, 151–153 Bermondsey Street,
London SE1 3HA

ISBN: 978-1-3988-4482-7
AD000168UK

Printed in China

INTRODUCTION

To set *The Egyptian Book of the Dead* in its wider context we need to remember that the civilization of ancient Egypt – the Egypt of the pharaohs – endured for well over 3,000 years before it came to an end with its annexation by Rome in around 30 BC. Periods of political strife and upheaval were balanced by times of peace and prosperity, the most significant of which coincide with the periods known as the Old Kingdom (2650–2152 BC), the Middle Kingdom (1986–1759 BC) and the New Kingdom (1539–1069 BC). It was during the New Kingdom that the Book of the Dead as we now know it emerged, but the ideas and beliefs expressed in it had gradually evolved

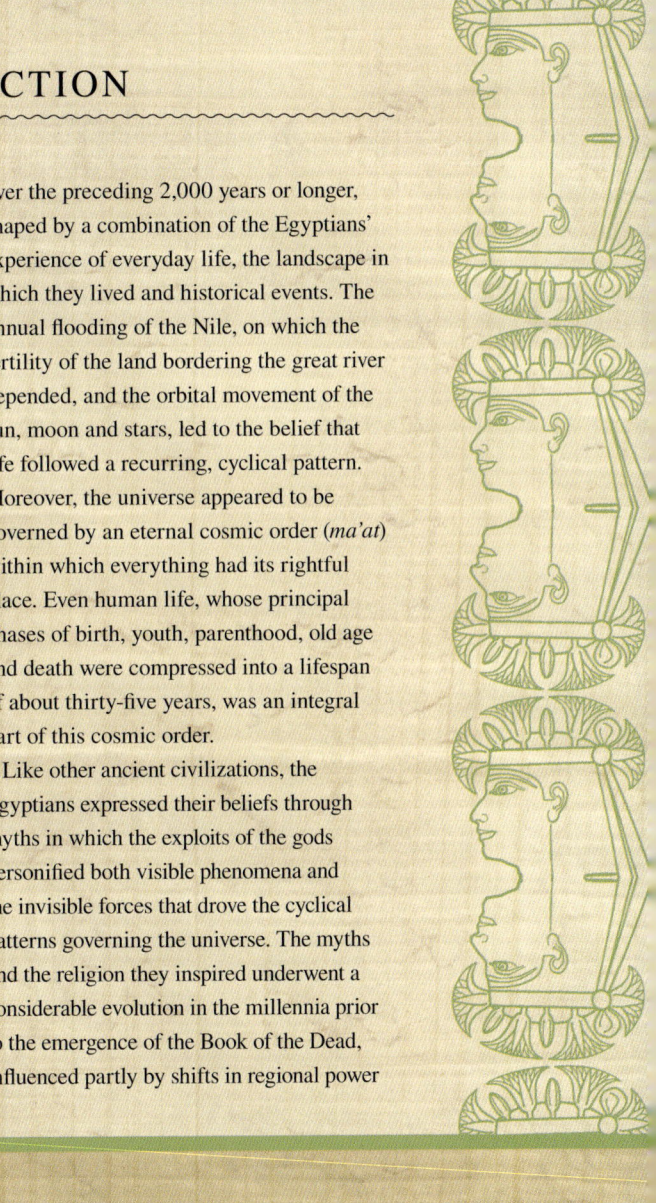

over the preceding 2,000 years or longer, shaped by a combination of the Egyptians' experience of everyday life, the landscape in which they lived and historical events. The annual flooding of the Nile, on which the fertility of the land bordering the great river depended, and the orbital movement of the sun, moon and stars, led to the belief that life followed a recurring, cyclical pattern. Moreover, the universe appeared to be governed by an eternal cosmic order (*ma'at*) within which everything had its rightful place. Even human life, whose principal phases of birth, youth, parenthood, old age and death were compressed into a lifespan of about thirty-five years, was an integral part of this cosmic order.

Like other ancient civilizations, the Egyptians expressed their beliefs through myths in which the exploits of the gods personified both visible phenomena and the invisible forces that drove the cyclical patterns governing the universe. The myths and the religion they inspired underwent a considerable evolution in the millennia prior to the emergence of the Book of the Dead, influenced partly by shifts in regional power

and partly by the priests who attended to the temples and cult centres in cities up and down the Nile. However, two elements remained constant: the prominence of the various gods associated with the sun (e.g. Ra, Horus and Aten) and the central role of the king or pharaoh. The latter made offerings to the gods on behalf of his subjects, and the gods reciprocated by giving life to the pharaoh and his people. According to the Book of the Dead, a similar reciprocal arrangement was believed to sustain the life of the deceased after his or her entombment.

Of the many myths left behind by the ancient Egyptians, there is one that is particularly relevant for the Book of the Dead – the myth of Osiris. The full myth is quite lengthy, but its principal elements are as follows. The sky-goddess Nut and the earth-god Geb had four children: two sons, Osiris and Set, and two daughters, Isis and Nephthys. The brothers married their sisters – Osiris married Isis, and Set married Nephthys – and Osiris, as first-born son, succeeded his father to the throne of Egypt. He ruled the primitive Egyptians with kindness and educated them, thus laying the foundations of the great civilization they were to become. Set grew jealous of Osiris and murdered him, dismembered his brother's body, scattered the pieces across Egypt and seated himself on the throne. Isis, with the help of her sister Nephthys and the gods Anubis and Thoth, located the pieces of her husband, gathered them together and mummified his body, thus restoring him to life. Rather than return to earth, however, Osiris became the eternal ruler of the realm of the afterlife, the Netherworld or Duat. Meanwhile Horus, the son of Osiris and Isis, avenged his father by defeating Set and becoming king in his father's place. From then on, the living pharaoh of Egypt embodied the spirit of Horus, while his deceased father became a new Osiris.

The Book of the Dead

The Book of the Dead grew out of a long tradition of funerary texts, the first examples of which are known as the Pyramid Texts because they were written on the walls of the burial chambers in the pyramids of the pharaohs of the Old Kingdom – the earliest known example was discovered in

the Pyramid of King Unas at Saqqara and dates from around 2345 BC. The purpose of the Pyramid Texts was to help the deceased pharaoh take his place among the gods, and to this end they included hymns, prayers and magical spells to ward off the dangers encountered in the afterlife. Initially they were exclusively for royal use but in the declining years of the Old Kingdom the right to use them was assumed by regional governors and other high-ranking officials, for they too wished to become identified with Osiris, who lived on as ruler of the Netherworld. A new corpus of funerary texts emerged during the Middle Kingdom – the Coffin Texts which, as their name implies, were written on the inner surfaces of wooden coffins. These texts included spells drawn from the Pyramid Texts plus many new compositions. Some of them also included illustrations. When coffins changed from rectangular wooden boxes to a shape that followed the contours of the mummified body, the texts were written on a papyrus which was rolled up and placed in the coffin with the deceased. Many thousands of these papyri were produced during the

New Kingdom, by which time the Book of the Dead had passed into widespread use. The title 'Book of the Dead' was first coined in 1842 by Richard Lepsius, the German Egyptologist, but it has been suggested that a more appropriate title would be 'Spells for Coming Forth by Day', for its purpose was to enable the deceased to emerge safely from the tomb in a perfected, spiritualized form. Nowadays the term 'Book of the Dead' usually refers to the entire corpus of almost 200 chapters or spells, from which a selection was made for inclusion in individual papyri. Although the format for presenting the selected chapters became more or less standardized, the order in which they were arranged varied from one papyrus to another.

Coming Forth By Day

The ancient Egyptians believed that the individual human being was a compound of several elements – the *kheperu*, meaning modes or manifestations of human existence – which disintegrated at death. These elements included the physical body (*khat*); the heart (*ib*), believed to be the seat of the mind or intelligence; the name (*ren*), which constituted

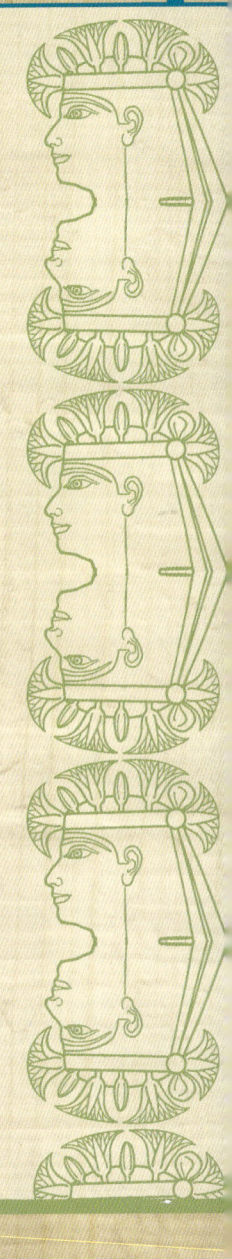

the individuality of the deceased and was thus essential for his or her continued existence in the afterlife; the shadow (*shut*), which was also related to the individuality of the deceased but was able to separate itself from the body and enjoy independent freedom of movement; the life-force or spirit (*ka*), which remained in the tomb with the body of the deceased and was nourished with a constant supply of offerings; the soul or spirit (*ba*), depicted in vignettes as a small bird with a human head, which was free to visit the world of the living during the day, returning to the tomb at sunset. The disintegration of these diverse elements was prevented through the mummification of the body, a process by which the deceased was transformed into a divine or spiritual form known as the *sah*.

When the mummy was placed in the tomb it was believed to enter the Duat or Netherworld, where it underwent two ceremonial rituals: the 'weighing of the heart' and the 'opening of the mouth'. The first of these was a form of judgement of the life of the deceased whereby his or her heart was placed in a scale and weighed against a feather, symbolizing *ma'at*. The ceremony was supervised by the jackal-headed Anubis and the ibis-headed Thoth, who wrote down the outcome. If the heart passed this test, the deceased could continue their passage through the Duat; if it failed, it was eaten by Ammit, the 'Devourer'. The second ritual, which was performed by a priest, involved touching the facial covering of the mummy with one or more ceremonial instruments, thereby 'unstopping' the mouth, eyes, ears and nostrils of the deceased so that they regained the use of these faculties. The opening of the mouth was of great importance since it enabled the deceased to recite the hymns and prayers written on the papyrus. It also enabled them to address by name the gods it would encounter in the Duat and respond correctly to their questioning.

Other items placed in the tomb with the mummy included the canopic jars (which contained the preserved internal organs of the deceased), a supply of offerings for the gods and the *ka*, and several small figures (*shabtis*) whose function was to help the deceased perform laborious tasks in the afterlife, such as ploughing the land in the Fields of Peace/Reeds.

If the deceased followed the instructions on the papyrus and recited its hymns and spells, they would become an *akh* (a blessed spirit) and, leaving the mummy in the tomb, they would join the gods Osiris and Ra.

The Papyrus of Ani

The papyrus of Ani, which dates from around 1275 BC, was found at Thebes and purchased by the British Museum in 1888. Ani was 'overseer of the double granary of the lord of Tawer', and his wife, Thuthu (or Tutu), was a chantress in the Temple of Amun. His papyrus is one of the longest known manuscripts of the Book of the Dead, measuring 23.5 metres (77 feet) in length, and contains over 60 chapters or spells. Many of these chapters are illustrated with richly coloured vignettes depicting the various stages of Ani's journey through the Duat towards the paradisal Field of Reeds. The majority of the text is written in black ink, while red ink is used for chapter headings and the instructions (rubrics) to be followed by the deceased. The papyrus begins with Ani, accompanied by his wife, offering praise to the sun-god Ra and to

Osiris, lord and ruler of the Duat. Subsequent vignettes show the ceremonies of the 'weighing of the heart' and the 'opening of the mouth'; Ani's funeral procession and the placing of his mummified body in the tomb; and his meetings with various gods in the course of his journey through the Duat. The papyrus culminates with Ani's arrival in the Fields of Peace (or Reeds).

The translation of the papyrus of Ani presented in the following pages is by E. A. Wallis Budge, Keeper of the Department of Egyptian and Assyrian Antiquities from 1894 to 1924. As well as enlarging the museum's Egyptian collections, Budge wrote many books that did much to stimulate popular interest in ancient Egypt. His translation of the payprus of Ani, which was published under the title of *The Egyptian Book of the Dead*, included many variant chapters from other manuscripts and numerous appendices, all of which have been omitted in this edition. He also inserted copious footnotes, some of which have been retained in shortened form alongside a few new ones.

John Baldock

PLATE 1

The scribe Ani, standing with hands raised in adoration before a table of offerings consisting of haunches of beef, loaves of bread and cake, vases of wine and oil, fruits, lotus, and other flowers. He wears a fringed white and saffron-coloured linen garment and has a wig, necklace, and bracelets. Behind him stands his wife 'Osiris, the lady of the house, the lady of the choir of Amun, Thuthu,' similarly robed and holding a sistrum and a branch in her right hand, and a *menat* in her left.[1]

1

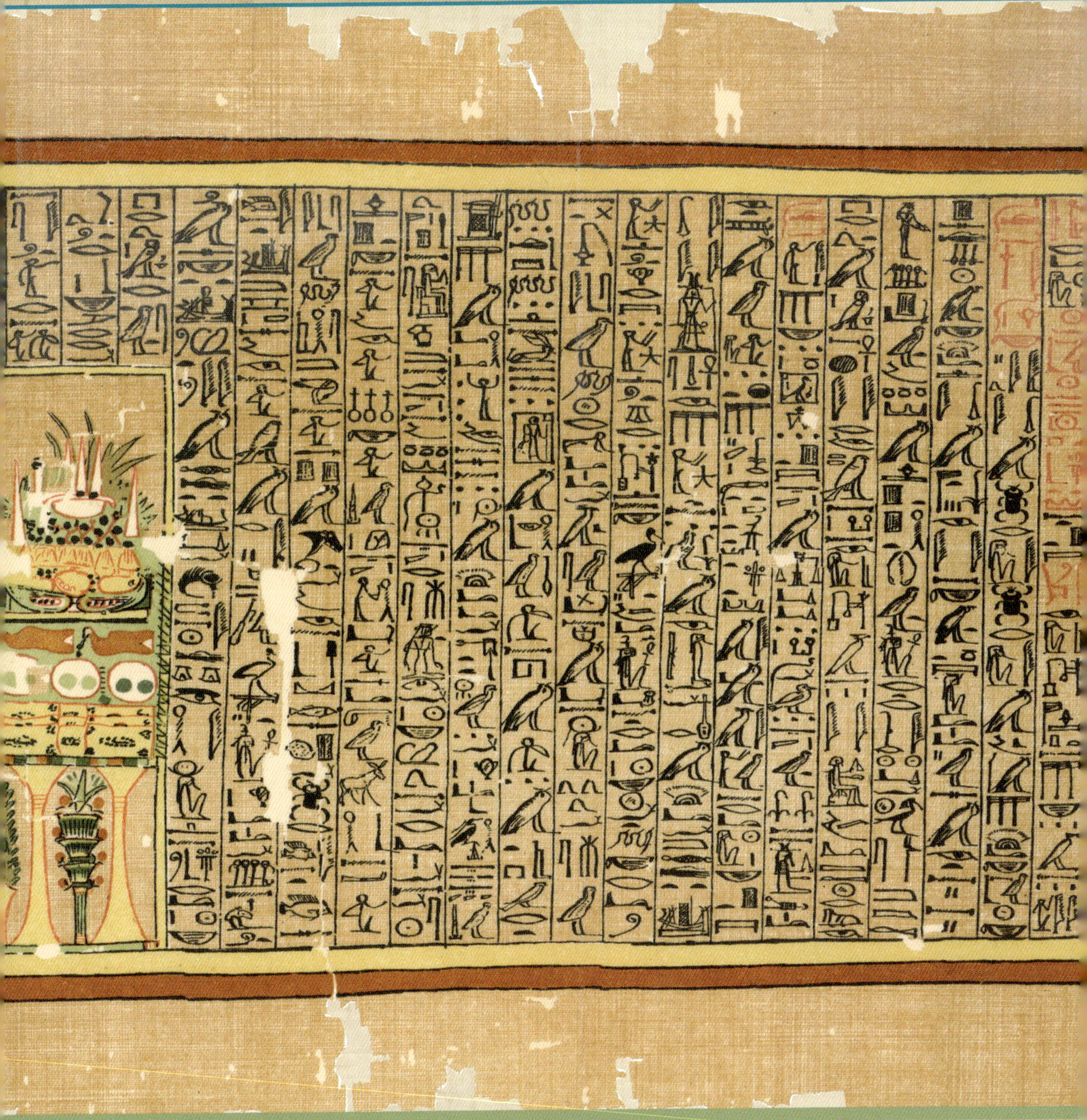

PLATE I

A HYMN OF PRAISE TO RA[2] WHEN HE RISETH IN THE EASTERN PART OF HEAVEN

Behold Osiris Ani the scribe who recordeth the holy offerings of all the gods, who saith: 'Homage to thee, O thou who hast come as Khepera,[3] Khepera, the creator of the gods. Thou risest, thou shinest, making bright thy mother [Nut],[4] crowned king of the gods. [Thy] mother Nut doeth homage unto thee with both her hands. The land of Manu[5] receiveth thee with content, and the goddess Maat[6] embraceth thee at the two seasons. May he give splendour, and power, and triumph, and a coming-forth as a living soul to see Horus of the two horizons to the ka *of Osiris,[7] the scribe Ani, triumphant before Osiris, who saith: Hail all ye gods of the Temple of the Soul, who weigh heaven and earth in the balance, and who provide food and abundance of meat. Hail Tatunen, One, creator of mankind and of the substance of the gods of the South and of the North, of the West and of the East. Ascribe [ye] praise unto Ra, the lord of heaven, the Prince, Life, Health, and Strength, the Creator of the gods, and adore ye him in his beautiful Presence as he riseth in the* atet[8] *boat. They who dwell in the heights and they who dwell in the depths worship thee. Thoth[9] and Maat both are thy recorders. Thine enemy[10] is given to the fire, the evil one hath fallen; his arms are bound, and his legs hath Ra taken from him. The children of impotent revolt shall never rise up again. The House*

PLATE 1   13

of the Prince[11] keepeth festival, and the sound of those who rejoice is in the mighty dwelling. The gods are glad [when] they see Ra in his rising; his beams flood the world with light. The majesty of the god, who is to be feared, setteth forth and cometh unto the land of Manu; he maketh bright the earth at his birth each day; he cometh unto the place where he was yesterday. O mayest thou be at peace with me; may I behold thy beauties; may I advance upon the earth; may I smite the Ass; may I crush the evil one; may I destroy Apep[12] in his hour; may I see the abtu fish at the time of his creation, and the ant fish in his creation, and the ant boat in its lake.[13] May I see Horus in charge of the rudder, with Thoth and Maat beside him; may I grasp the bows of the seket boat,[14] and the stern of the atet boat. May he grant unto the ka of Osiris Ani to behold the disk of the Sun and to see the Moon-god without ceasing, every day; and may my soul come forth and walk hither and thither and whithersoever it pleaseth. May my name be proclaimed when it is found upon the board of the table of offerings; may offerings be made unto me in my presence, even as they are made unto the followers of Horus; may there be prepared for me a seat in the boat of the Sun on the day of the going forth of the god; and may I be received into the presence of Osiris in the land of triumph!'

PLATE 2

The disk of the Sun, supported by a pair of arms proceeding from the *ankh*, the sign of life, which in turn is supported by a *tet*, the emblem of the East and of the god Osiris. The *tet* stands upon the horizon. On each side of the disk are three dog-headed apes, spirits of the Dawn, their arms raised in adoration of the disk. On the right-hand side of the *tet* is the goddess Nephthys and on the left is Isis, each goddess raising her hands in adoration of the *tet*, and kneeling upon the emblem *aat*, or hemisphere. Above is the sky. This vignette belongs properly to the hymn to the rising sun.

HYMN TO OSIRIS

Glory be to Osiris Un-nefer, the great god within Abydos, king of eternity, lord of the everlasting, who passeth through millions of years in his existence. Eldest son of the womb of Nut, engendered by Seb the Erpat, lord of the crowns of the North and South, lord of the lofty white crown. As prince of gods and of men he hath received the crook and the flail and the dignity of his divine fathers.[15] Let thy heart which is in the mountain of Amenta[16] be content, for thy son Horus is stablished upon thy throne. Thou art crowned lord of Tattu and ruler in Abtu.[17] Through thee the world waxeth

green in triumph before the might of Neb-er-tcher.[18] He leadeth in his train that which is and that which is not yet, in his name Ta-her-seta-nef;[19] he toweth along the earth in triumph in his name Seker.[20] He is exceeding mighty and most terrible in his name Osiris. He endureth for ever and for ever in his name Un-nefer.[21] Homage to thee, King of kings, Lord of lords,

2

PLATE 2   15

Prince of princes, who from the womb of Nut hast possessed the world and hast ruled all lands and Akert.[22] Thy body is of gold, thy head is of azure, and emerald light encircleth thee. O An[23] of millions of years, all-pervading with thy body and beautiful in countenance in Ta-sert. Grant thou to the ka of Osiris, the scribe Ani, splendour in heaven and might upon earth and triumph in Neter-khert; and that I may sail down to Tattu like a living soul and up to Abtu like a bennu (phœnix); and that I may go in and come out without repulse at the pylons of the Tuat. May there be given unto me loaves of bread in the house of coolness, and offerings of food in Annu, and a homestead for ever in Sekhet-Aru[24] with wheat and barley there for.'

PLATE 3

Scene of the Weighing of the Heart of the Dead. Ani and his wife enter the Hall of Double Law or Truth, wherein the heart, emblematical of the conscience, is to be weighed in the balance against the feather, emblematical of law. Above, twelve gods, each holding a sceptre, are seated upon thrones before a table of offerings of fruit, flowers, etc. Their names are: Harmachis, 'the great god within his boat'; Tmu; Shu; Tefnut, 'lady of heaven'; Seb; Nut, 'lady of heaven'; Isis; Nephthys; Horus, 'the great god'; Hathor, 'lady of Amenta'; and Sa. Upon the beam of the scales sits the dog-headed ape that was associated with Thoth, the scribe of the gods. The god Anubis, jackal-headed, 3

PLATE 3　　　　　　　　　　　　17

tests the tongue of the balance, the suspending bracket of which is in the form of the feather. The inscription above the head of Anubis reads: 'He who is in the tomb saith, "pray thee, O weigher of righteousness, to guide (?) the balance that it may be stablished"'. On the left of the balance, facing Anubis, stands Ani's 'Luck' or 'Destiny', *Shai*, and above is the object called *meskhen*, which has been described as 'a cubit with human head' and which is supposed to be connected with the place of birth. Behind these stand the goddesses Meskhenet and Renenet: Meskhenet presiding over the birth-chamber, and Renenet probably superintending the rearing of children. Behind the *meskhen* is the soul of Ani in the form of a human-headed bird standing on a pylon. On the right of the balance, behind Anubis, stands Thoth, the scribe of the gods, with his reed-pen and palette containing black and red ink, with which to record the result of the trial. Behind Thoth stands the female monster Amam, the 'Devourer', or Ammit, the 'eater of the dead'.[25]

Osiris, the scribe Ani, saith: 'My heart my mother, my heart my mother, my heart my coming into being! May there be nothing to resist me at [my] judgment; may there be no opposition to me from the Tchatcha;[26] may there be no parting of thee from me in the presence of him who keepeth the scales! Thou art my ka within my body [which] knitteth and strengtheneth my limbs. Mayest thou come forth to the place of happiness to which I am advancing. May the Shenit[27] not cause my name to stink, and may no lies be spoken against me in the presence of the god! Good is it for thee to hear...'[28]

Thoth, the righteous judge of the great company of the gods who are in the presence of the god Osiris, saith: 'Hear ye this judgment. The heart of Osiris hath in very truth been weighed, and his soul hath stood as a witness for him; it hath been found true by trial in the Great Balance. There hath not been found any wickedness in him; he hath not wasted the offerings in the temples; he hath not done harm by his deeds; and he uttered no evil reports while he was upon earth.'

The great company of the gods reply to Thoth dwelling in Khemennu: 'That which cometh forth from thy mouth hath been ordained. Osiris, the scribe Ani, triumphant, is holy and righteous. He hath not sinned, neither hath he done evil against us. Let it not be given to the devourer Ammit to prevail over him. Meat-offerings and entrance into the presence of the god Osiris shall be granted unto him, together with a homestead for ever in Sekhet-hetepu, as unto the followers of Horus.'

PLATE 3   19

PLATE 4

Ani, found just, is led into the presence of Osiris. On the left the hawk-headed god Horus, the son of Isis, wearing the double crown of the North and the South, takes Ani by the hand and leads him forward towards Osiris, the 'lord of eternity', who is enthroned on the right within a shrine in the form of a funereal chest. The god wears the *atef* crown with plumes; a *menat* hangs from the back of his neck; and he holds in his hands the crook, sceptre, and flail, emblems of sovereignty and dominion. He is wrapped in bandages ornamented with scale work. The side of his throne is painted to resemble the doors of the tomb. Behind him stand Nephthys on his right hand and Isis on his left. Facing him, and standing on a lotus flower, are the four 'children of Horus (or Osiris)', or gods of the cardinal points. The first, Mestha, has the head of a man; the second, Hapi, the head of an ape; the third, Tuamautef, the head

of a jackal; and the fourth, Qebhsennuf, the head of a hawk. Suspended near the lotus is an object which is usually called a panther's skin, but is more probably a bullock's hide.

The roof of the shrine is supported on pillars with lotus capitals, and is surmounted by a figure of Horus-Sept or Horus-Seker and rows of uraei.[29]

In the centre Ani kneels before the god upon a reed mat, raising his right hand in adoration, and holding in his left hand the *kherp* sceptre. He wears a whitened wig surmounted by a 'cone', the significance of which is unknown. Round his neck is a deep collar of precious stones. Near him stands a table of offerings of meat, fruit, flowers, etc., and in the compartments above are a number of vessels for wine, beer, oil, wax, etc., together with bread, cakes, ducks, a wreath, and single flowers.

PLATE 4   21

4

Saith Horus, the son of Isis: 'I have come unto thee, O Unnefer, and I have brought the Osiris Ani unto thee. His heart is [found] righteous coming forth from the balance, and it hath not sinned against god or goddess. Thoth hath weighed it according to the decree uttered unto him by the company of the gods; and it is very true and righteous. Grant him cakes and ale; and let him enter into the presence of Osiris; and may he be like unto the followers of Horus for ever.'

Behold, Osiris Ani saith: 'O Lord of Amentet (the underworld), I am in thy presence. There is no sin in me, I have not lied wittingly, nor have I done aught with a false heart. Grant that I may be like unto those favoured ones who are round about thee, and that I may be an Osiris, greatly favoured of the beautiful god and beloved of the lord of the world, the royal scribe indeed, who loveth him Ani, triumphant before the god Osiris.'

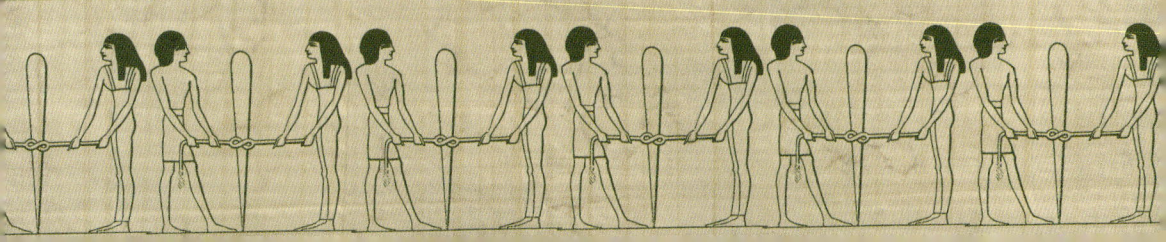

The funereal procession to the tomb, running the length of Plates 5 and 6. In the centre of Plate 5, the mummy of the dead man is seen lying in a chest or shrine mounted on a boat with runners, which is drawn by oxen. In the boat, at the head and foot of the mummy, are two small models of Nephthys and Isis. By the side kneels Ani's wife Thuthu, lamenting. In front of the boat is the *Sem* priest[30] burning incense in a censer and pouring out a libation from a vase; he wears his characteristic dress, a panther's skin. Eight mourners follow, one of whom has his hair whitened. In the rear a sepulchral ark or chest,[31] surmounted by a figure of Anubis and ornamented with emblems of protection and stability, is drawn on a sledge by four attendants, and is followed by two others. By their side walk other attendants carrying Ani's palette, boxes, chair, couch, staff, etc.

In Plate 6 (see pages 26–7), the procession is continued up to the tomb. In the centre is a group of wailing women, followed by attendants carrying on yokes boxes of flowers, vases of unguents, etc. To the right of centre are a cow with her calf, chairs of painted wood with flowers upon them, and an attendant with shaven head, carrying a haunch, newly cut, for the funereal feast. The group on the right is performing the last rites. Before the door of the tomb stands the mummy of Ani to receive the final honours; behind him, embracing him, stands Anubis, the god of the tomb; and at his feet, in front, kneels Thuthu to bid a last farewell to her husband's body. Before a table of offerings stand two priests: the *Sem* priest, who wears a panther's skin, holding in his right hand a libation vase, and in his left a censer; and a priest holding in his right hand an instrument[32]

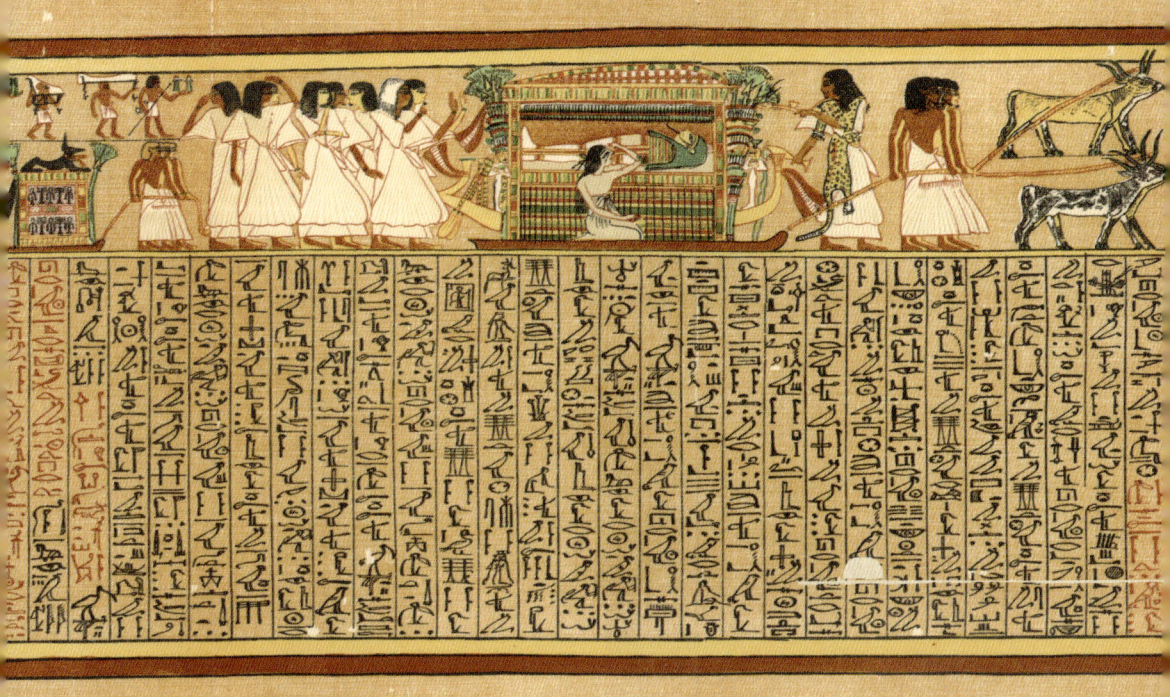

5

with which he is about to touch the mouth and eyes of the mummy, and in his left the instrument for 'opening the mouth'. Behind or beside them on the ground, in a row, lie the instruments employed in the ceremony of 'opening the mouth', etc., the *mesxet* instrument, the sepulchral box, the boxes of purification, the bandlet, the libation vases, the ostrich feather and the instruments called *Seb-ur*, *Temanu* or *Tun-tet*, and the *Pesh-en-kef*. The *Kher-heb* priest stands behind, reading the service of the dead from a papyrus.

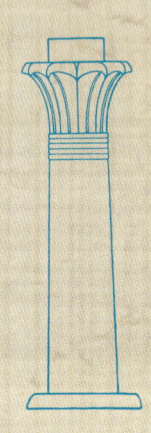

HERE BEGIN THE CHAPTERS OF COMING
FORTH BY DAY, AND OF THE SONGS OF
PRAISE AND GLORIFYING, AND OF COMING
FORTH FROM AND GOING INTO THE
GLORIOUS NETER-KHERT IN THE BEAUTIFUL
AMENTA; TO BE SAID ON THE DAY OF THE
BURIAL: GOING IN AFTER COMING FORTH.
*Osiris Ani, Osiris, the scribe Ani, saith:
'Homage to thee, O bull of Amenta, Thoth the
king of eternity is with me. I am the great god
in the boat of the Sun; I have fought for thee.
I am one of the gods, those holy princes[33] who
make Osiris to be victorious over his enemies
on the day of weighing of words. I am thy
mediator, O Osiris. I am [one] of the gods born
of Nut, those who slay the foes of Osiris and
hold for him in bondage the fiend Sebau. I am
thy mediator, O Horus. I have fought for thee, I
have put to flight the enemy for thy name's sake.
I am Thoth, who have made Osiris victorious*

*over his enemies on the day of weighing of
words in the great House of the mighty Ancient
One in Annu.[34] I am Tetteti,[35] the son of Tetteti;
I was conceived in Tattu, I was born in Tattu. I
am with those who weep and with the women
who bewail Osiris in the double land (?) of
Rechtet; and I make Osiris to be victorious over
his enemies. Ra commanded Thoth to make
Osiris victorious over his enemies; and that
which was bidden for me Thoth did. I am with
Horus on the day of the clothing of Teshtesh[36]
and of the opening of the storehouses of water
for the purification of the god whose heart
moveth not, and of the unbolting of the door
of concealed things in Re-stau.[37] I am with
Horus who guardeth the left shoulder of Osiris
in Sekhem,[38] and I go into and come out from
the divine flames on the day of the destruction
of the fiends in Sekhem. I am with Horus on
the day of the festivals of Osiris, making the*

offerings on the sixth day of the festival, [and on] the Tenat festival in Annu. I am a priest in Tattu, Rere (?) in the temple of Osiris, [on the day of] casting up the earth.[39] I see the things which are concealed in Re-stau. I read from the book of the festival of the Soul [which is] in Tattu. I am the Sem priest, and I perform his course. I am the great chief of the work[40] on the day of the placing of the hennu boat of Seker upon its sledge.[41] I have grasped the spade on the day of digging the ground in Suten-henen. O ye who make perfected souls to enter into the Hall of Osiris, may ye cause the perfected soul of Osiris, the scribe Ani, victorious [in the Hall of Double Truth], to enter with you into the house of Osiris. May he hear as ye hear; may he see as ye see; may he stand as ye stand; may he sit as ye sit!

'O ye who give bread and ale to perfected souls in the Hall of Osiris, give ye bread and ale at the two seasons to the soul of Osiris Ani, who is victorious before all the gods of Abtu, and who is victorious with you.

'O ye who open the way and lay open the paths to perfected souls in the Hall of Osiris, open ye the way and lay open the paths to the soul of Osiris, the scribe and steward of all the divine offerings, Ani [who is triumphant] with you. May he enter in with a bold heart and may he come forth in peace from the house of Osiris. May he not be rejected, may he not be turned back, may he enter in [as he] pleaseth, may he come forth [as he] desireth, and may he be victorious. May his bidding be done in the house of Osiris; may he walk, and may he speak with you, and may he be a glorified soul along with you. He hath not been found wanting there, and the Balance is rid of [his] trial.'

CHAPTER OF GIVING A MOUTH TO OSIRIS ANI, THE SCRIBE AND TELLER OF THE HOLY OFFERINGS OF ALL THE GODS. MAY HE BE VICTORIOUS IN NETER-KHERT!

'I rise out of the egg in the hidden land. May my mouth be given unto me that I may speak with it before the great god, the lord of the underworld. May my hand and my arm not be forced back by the holy ministers of any god. I am Osiris, the lord of the mouth of the tomb; and Osiris, the victorious scribe Ani, hath a portion with him who is upon the top of the steps. According to the desire of my heart, I have come from the Pool of Fire, and I have quenched it. Homage to thee, O thou lord of brightness, thou who art at the head of the Great House, and who dwellest in night and in thick darkness; I have come unto thee. I am glorious, I am pure; my arms support thee. Thy portion shall be with those who have gone before. O grant unto me my mouth that I may speak therewith; and that I may follow my heart when it passeth through the fire and darkness.'

Rubric: If this writing be known [by the deceased] upon earth, and this chapter be done into writing upon [his] coffin, he shall come forth by day in all the forms of existence which he desireth, and he shall enter into [his] place and shall not be rejected. Bread and ale and meat shall be given unto Osiris, the scribe Ani, upon the altar of Osiris. He shall enter into the Fields of Aaru in peace, to learn the bidding of him who dwelleth in Tattu; there shall wheat and barley be given unto him; there shall he flourish as he did upon earth; and he shall do whatsoever pleaseth him, even as [do] the gods who are in the underworld, for everlasting millions of ages, world without end.

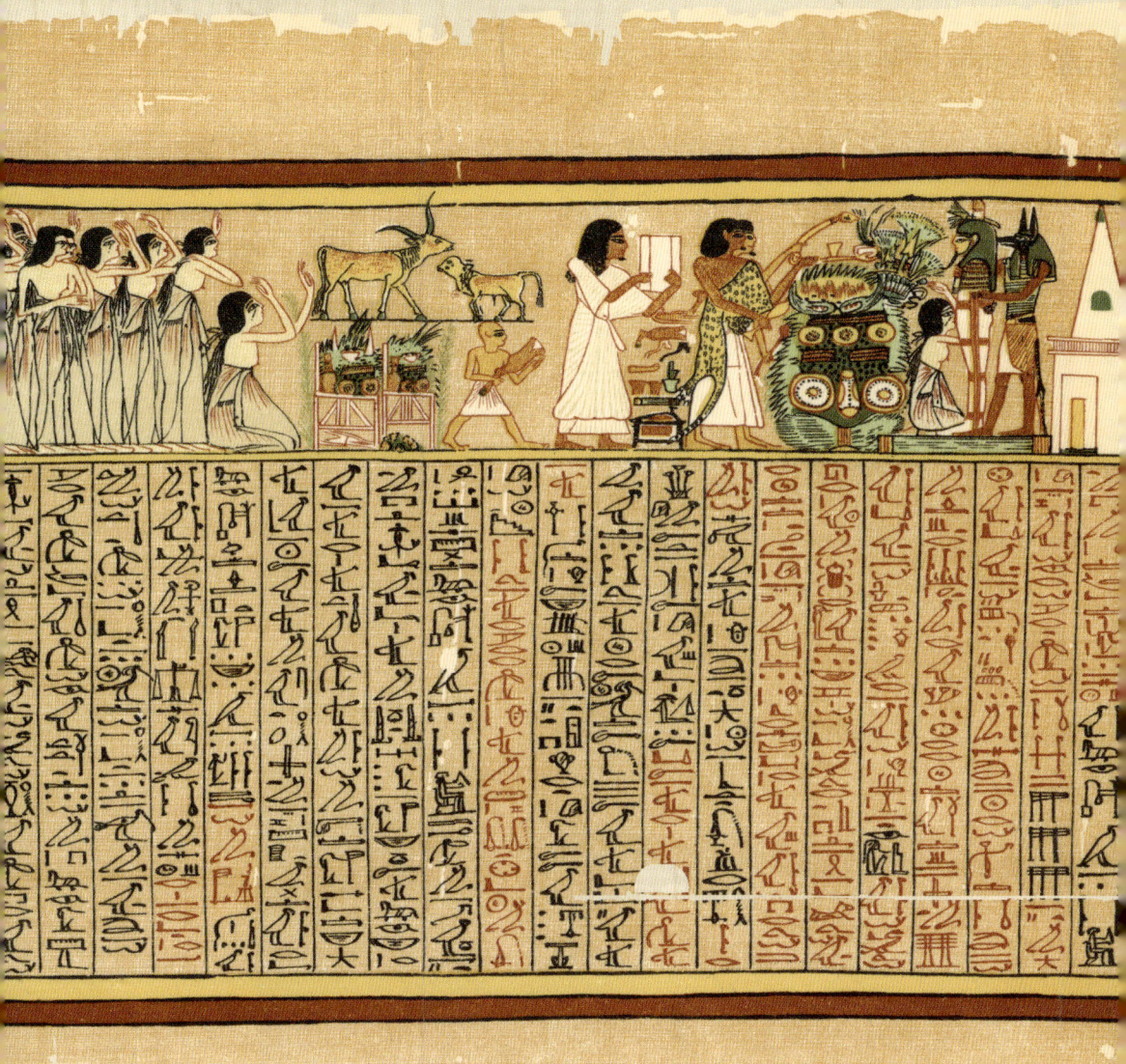

PLATES 7-10

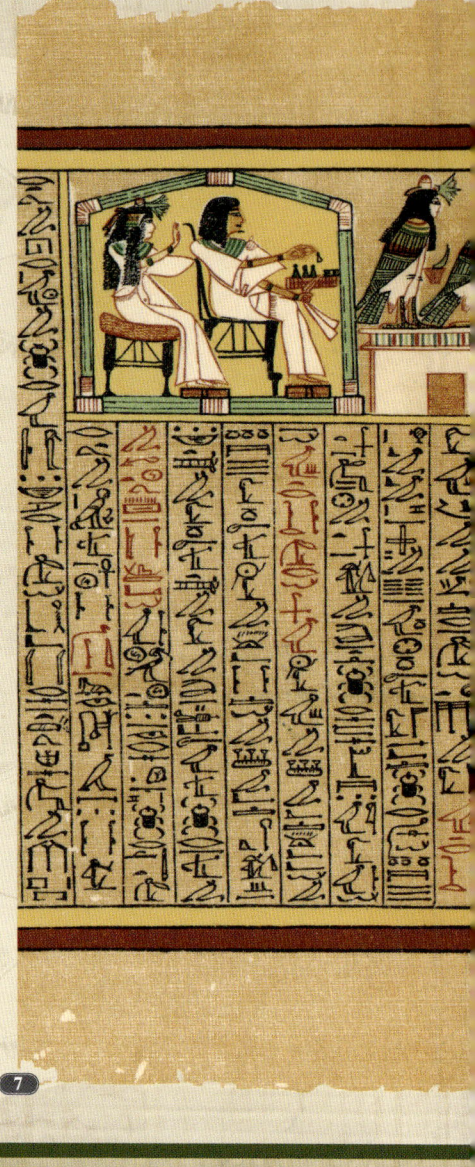

The vignette of these plates, forming one composition, runs along the top of the text. The subjects are listed next to each plate:

PLATE 7

1. Ani and his wife in the *seh* hall; he is moving a piece on a draught board.

2. The souls of Ani and his wife standing upon a pylon-shaped building. The hieroglyphics by the side of Ani's soul read 'the soul of Osiris'.

3. A table of offerings, upon which are laid a libation vase, plants, and lotus flowers.

4. Two lions seated back to back and supporting the horizon, over which extends the sky. The lion on the right is called 'Yesterday', and that on the left 'Tomorrow'.

5. The *bennu* bird,[42] and a table of offerings.

6. The mummy of Ani lying on a bier within a funereal shrine; the head and foot are Nephthys and Isis in the form of hawks. Beneath the bier are vases painted to imitate variegated marble or glass, a funereal box, Ani's palette, etc.

7

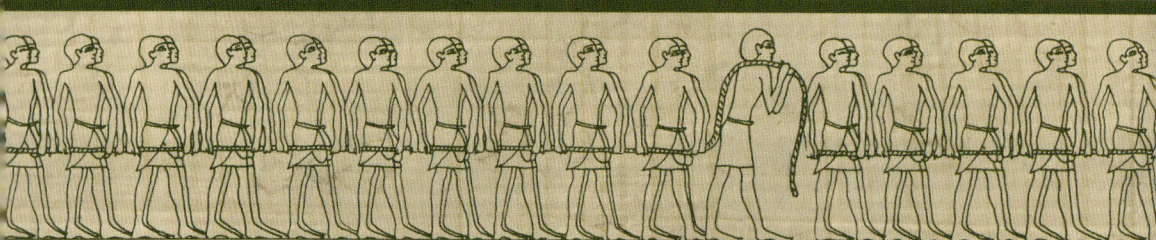

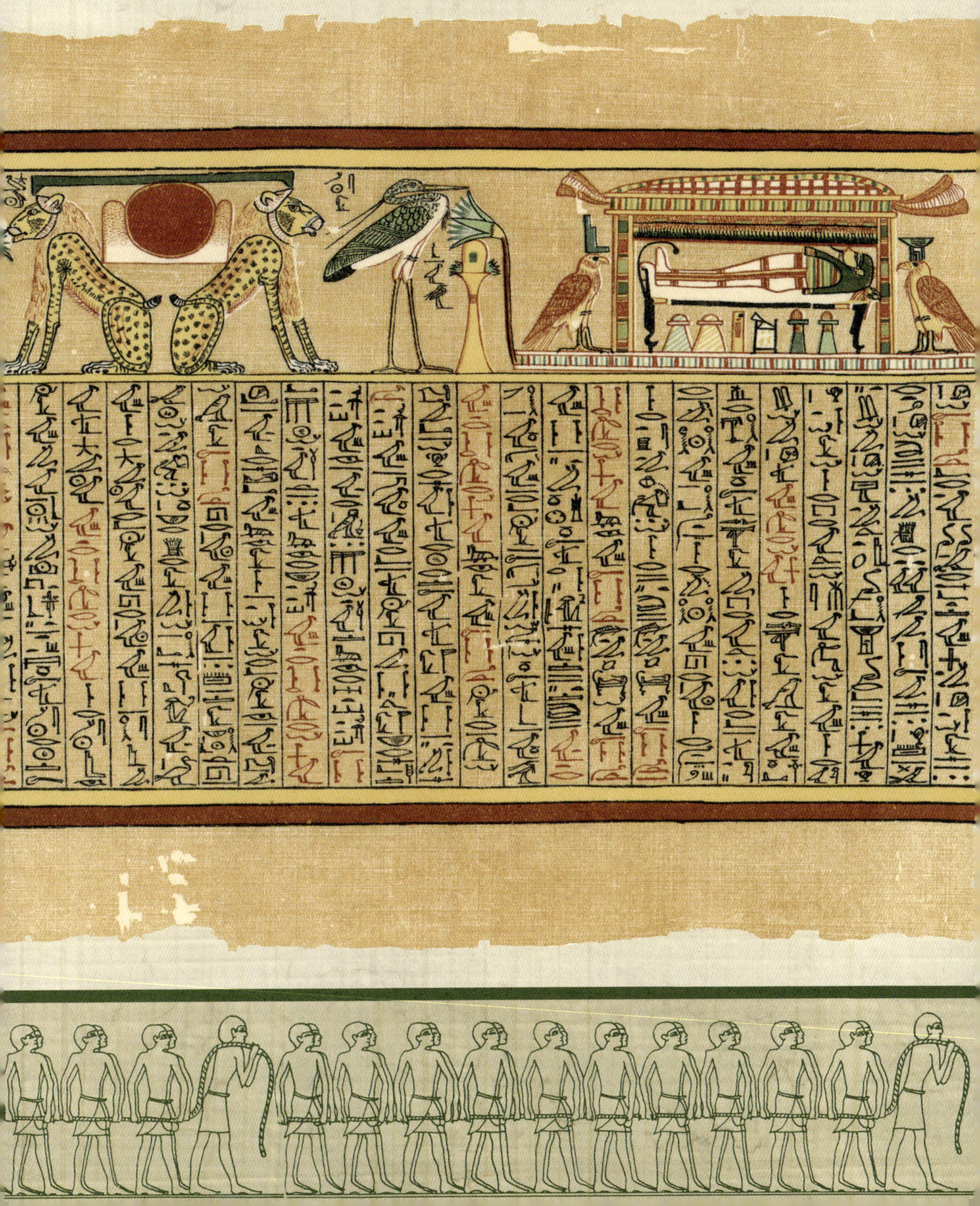

PLATE 8

 **1.** The god Heh, 'Millions of years', wearing the emblem of 'years' upon his head, and holding a similar object in his right hand; he is kneeling and extends his left hand over a pool (?) in which is an eye.

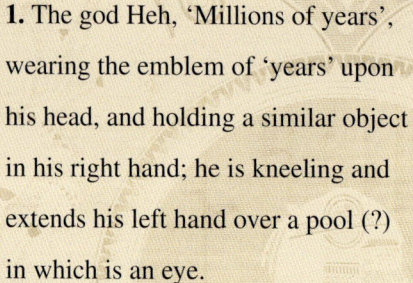 **2.** The god Uatch-ura, 'Great Green Water,' with each hand extended over a pool; the one under his right hand is called She en hesmen, 'Pool of Natron', and the one under his left hand is She en Maaat, 'Pool of Nitre' (or Salt).

 **3.** A pylon with doors, called Re-stau, 'Gate of the funereal passages'.

 **4.** The *utchat* facing to the left above a pylon.[43]

 **5.** The cow Mehurt Maat Ra, 'Mehurt, the eye of Ra', with a flail and having on her head a disk and horns and round her neck the collar and *menat*.

 **6.** A funereal chest from which emerges the head of Ra and his two arms and hands, each holding the emblem of life. The chest, which is called aat Abtu, 'the district of Abydos,' or the 'burial place of the East,' has upon its side figures of the four children of Horus who protect the intestines of Osiris or the deceased. On the right stand Tuamautef and Qebhsennuf, and on the left, Mestha and Hapi.

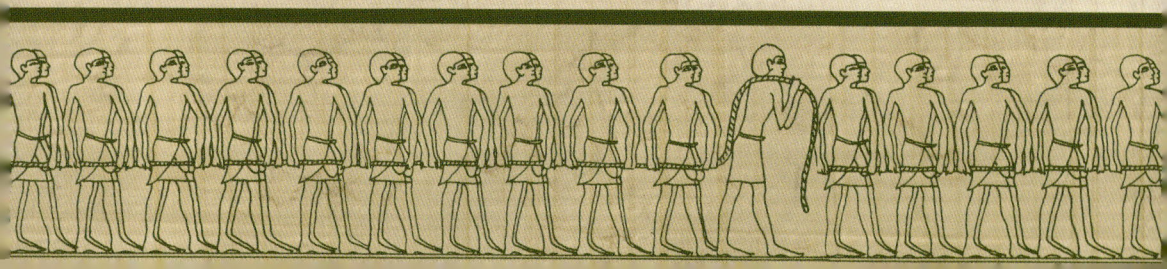

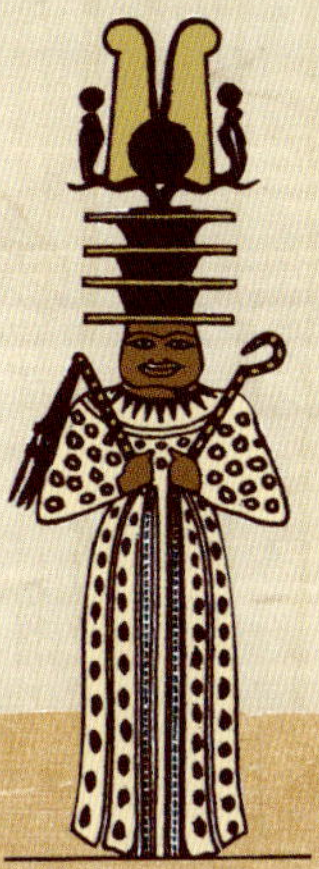

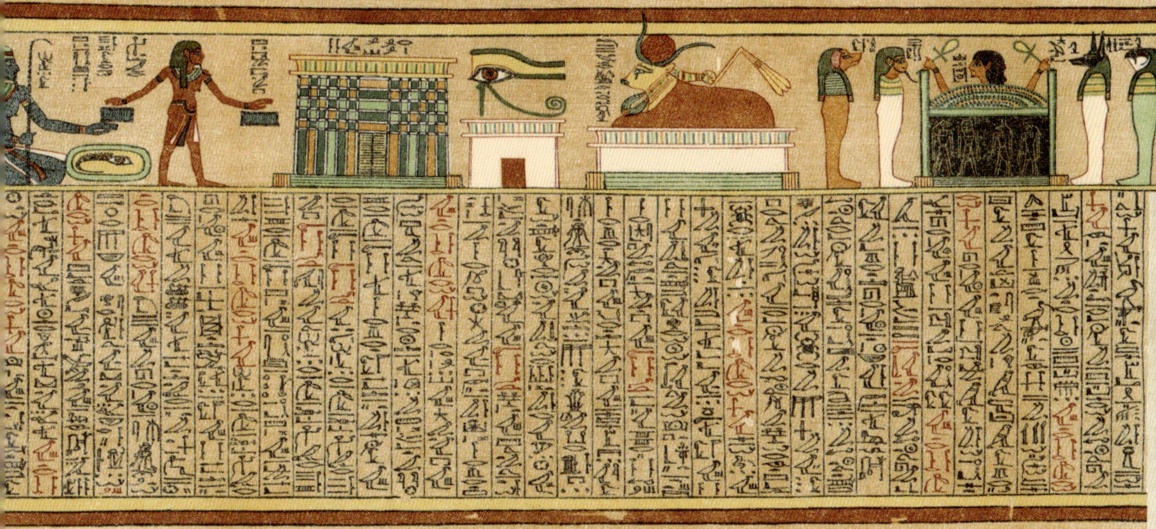

8

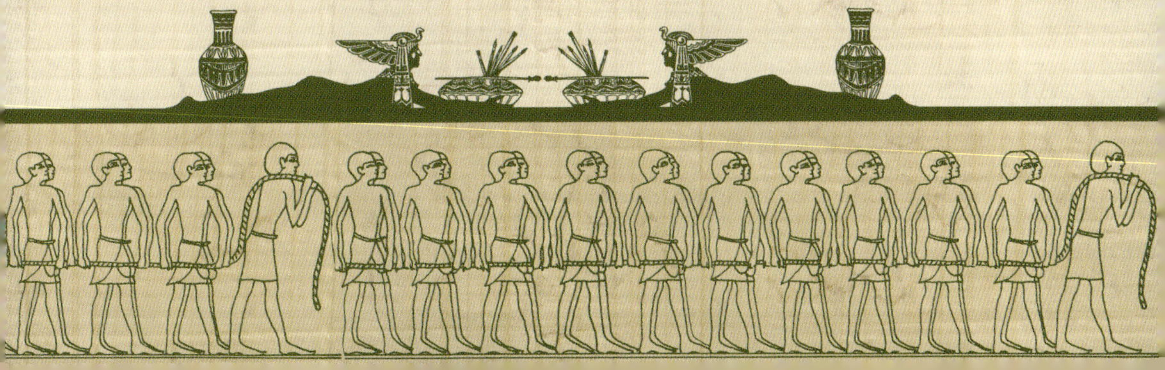

PLATE 9

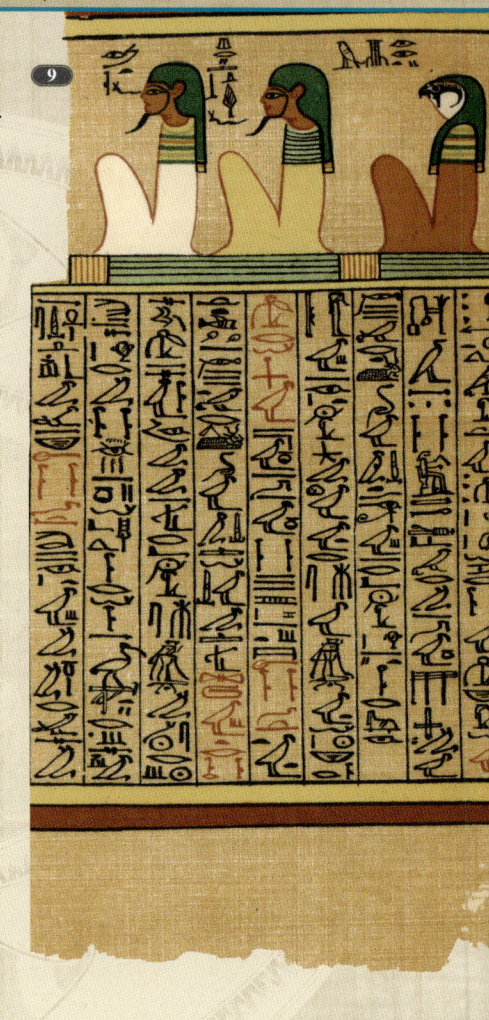

9

1. Figures of three gods who, together with Mestha, Hapi, Tuamautef, and Qebhsennuf, are the 'seven shining ones'. Their names are: Maa-atef-f, Kheri-beq-f, and Heru-khent-Maati.

2. The god Anpu (Anubis), jackal-headed.

3. Figures of seven gods, whose names are Netchehnetcheh, Aaqetqet, Khenti-heh-f,[44] Ami-unnut-f,[45] Tesher-maa,[46] Bes-maa-em-kerh,[47] and An-em-hru.[48]

4. The soul of Ra, and the soul of Osiris in the form of a human-headed bird wearing the crown conversing in Tattu.

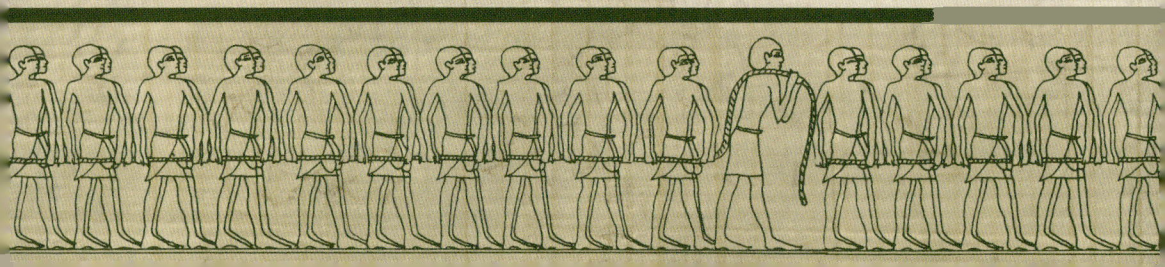

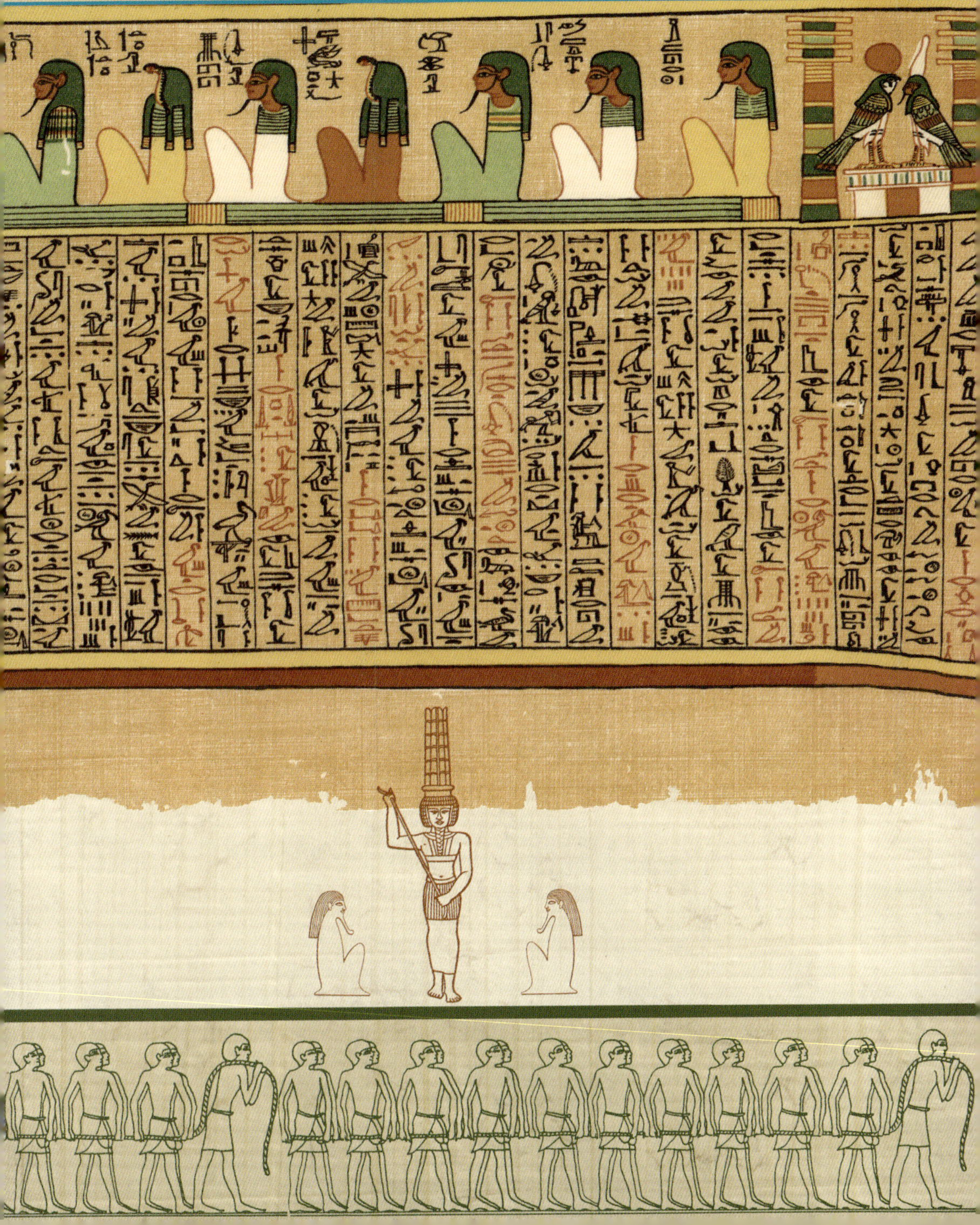

PLATE 10

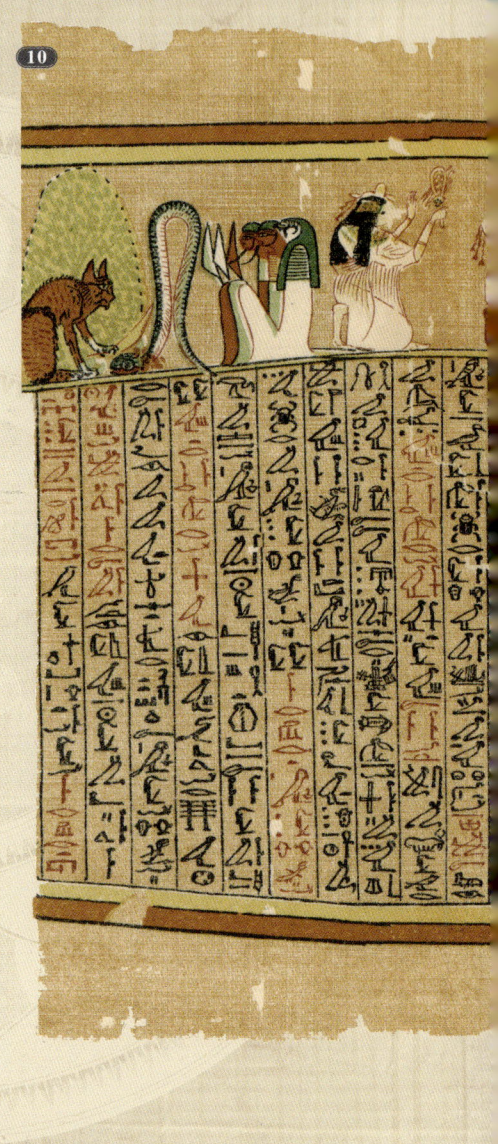

1. The Cat (i.e. the Sun), which dwells by the Persea tree in Heliopolis, cutting off the head of the serpent Apepi, emblematic of his enemies.

2. Three seated deities holding knives. They are probably Sau, Horus of Sekhem, and Nefer-Tmu.

3. Ani and his wife Thuthu, who holds a sistrum, kneeling in adoration before the god Khepera, beetle-headed, who is seated in the boat of the rising sun.

4. Two apes, emblematic of Isis and Nephthys.

5. The god Tmu, seated within the Sun-disk in the boat of the setting sun, facing a table of offerings.

6. The god Rehu, in the form of a lion.

7. The serpent Uatchit, the lady of flame, a symbol of the eye of Ra, coiled round a lotus flower. Above is the emblem of fire.

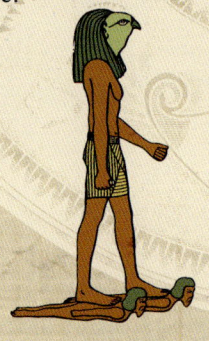

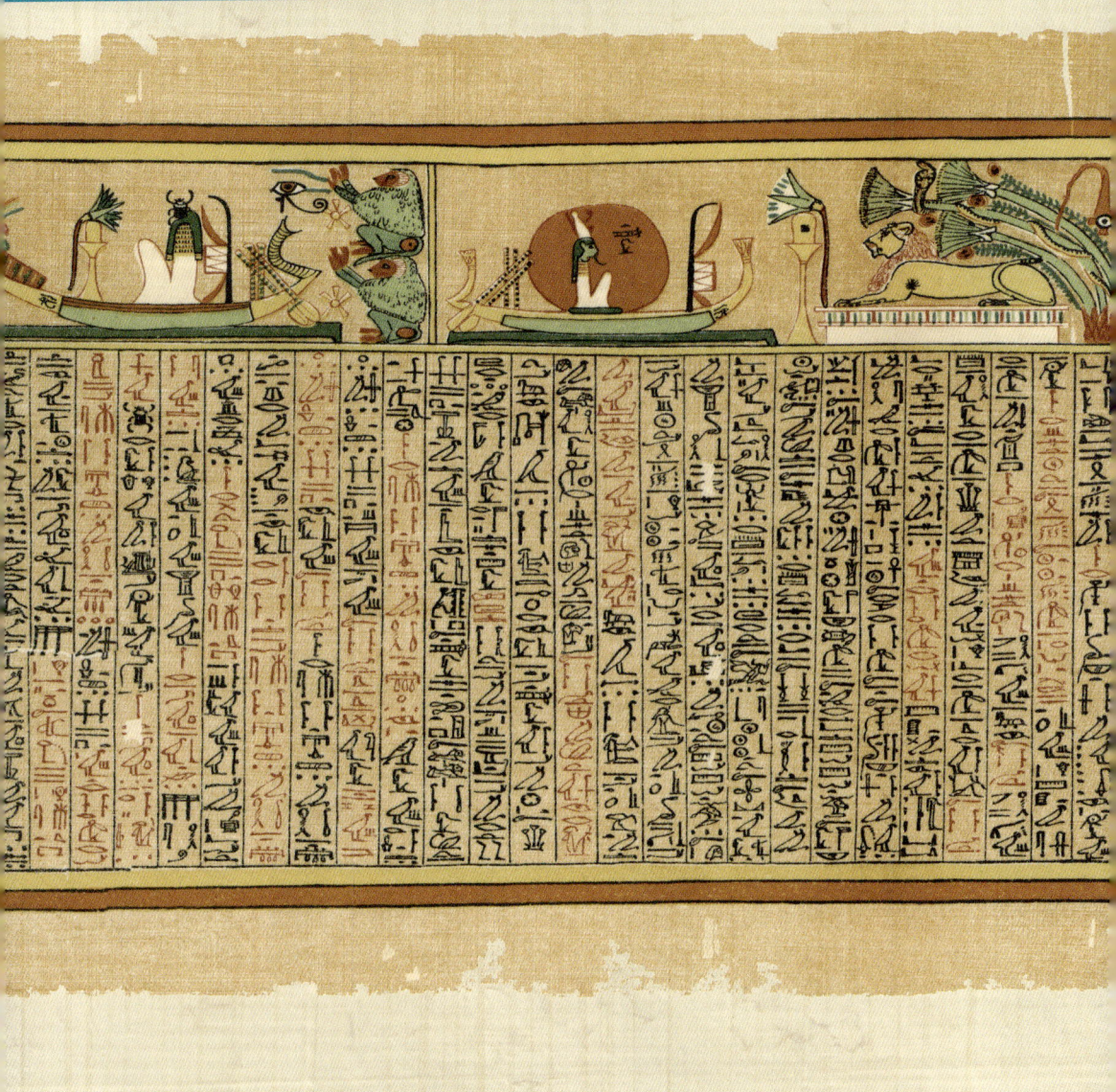

TEXT FOR PLATES 7–10

HERE BEGIN THE PRAISES AND
GLORIFYINGS OF COMING OUT FROM
AND GOING INTO THE GLORIOUS NETER-
KHERT IN THE BEAUTIFUL AMENTA, OF
COMING OUT BY DAY IN ALL THE FORMS
OF EXISTENCE WHICH PLEASE HIM (I.E.
THE DECEASED), OF PLAYING AT DRAUGHTS
AND SITTING IN THE SEH HALL, AND OF
COMING FORTH AS A LIVING SOUL.

*Behold Osiris, the scribe Ani, after he hath come
to his haven [of rest]. That which hath been done
upon earth [by Ani] being blessed, all the words
of the god Tmu come to pass. 'I am the god Tmu
in [my] rising;*[49] *I am the only One. I came into
existence in Nu. I am Ra who rose in the beginning.'*

*Who then is this? It is Ra who rose for the
first time in the city of Suten-henen [crowned]
as a king in [his] rising. The pillars of Shu*[50]
*were not as yet created, when he was upon
the high place of him who is in Khemennu.*

*'I am the great god who gave birth to
himself, even Nu, [who] created his name*

Paut Neteru[51] *as god.'*

*Who then is this? It is Ra, the creator of the
name[s] of his limbs, which came into being in
the form of the gods in the train of Ra.*

*'I am he who is not driven back among
the gods.'*

*Who then is this? It is Tmu in his disk, or
(as others say), It is Ra in his rising in the
eastern horizon of heaven.*

'I am Yesterday; I know Tomorrow.'

*Who then is this? Yesterday is Osiris, and
Tomorrow is Ra, on the day when he shall
destroy the enemies of Neb-er-tcher, and
when he shall stablish as prince and ruler his
son Horus, or (as others say), on the day
when we commemorate the festival of the
meeting of the dead Osiris with his father Ra,
and when the battle of the gods was fought in
which Osiris, lord of Amentet, was the leader.*

*What then is this? It is Amentet, [that is
to say] the creation of the souls of the gods
when Osiris was leader in Set-Amentet; or*

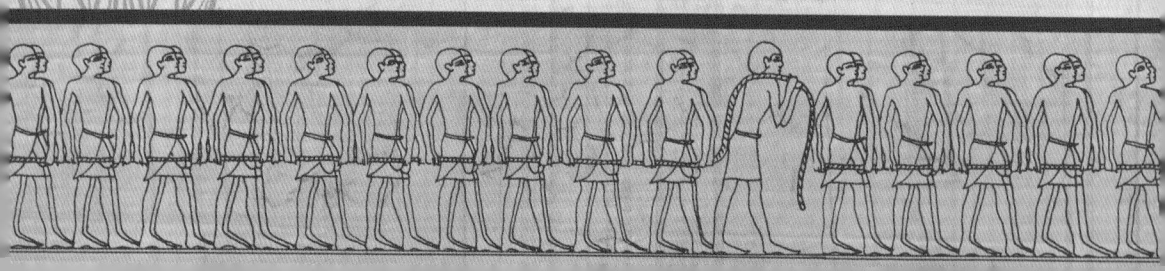

(as others say), Amentet is that which Ra hath given unto me; when any god cometh, he doth arise and doeth battle for it.

'I know the god who dwelleth therein.'

Who then is this? It is Osiris, or (as others say), Ra is his name, even Ra the self-created.

'I am the bennu bird which is in Annu, and I am the keeper of the volume of the book of things[52] which are and of things which shall be.'

Who then is this? It is Osiris, or (as others say), It is his dead body, or (as others say), It is his filth. The things which are and the things which shall be are his dead body; or (as others say), They are eternity and everlastingness. Eternity is the day, and everlastingness is the night.

'I am the god Amsu[53] in his coming-forth; may his two plumes be set upon my head.'

Who then is this? Amsu is Horus, the avenger of his father, and his coming-forth is his birth. The plumes upon his head are Isis and Nephthys when they go forth to set themselves there, even as his protectors, and they provide

that which his head lacketh, or (as others say), They are the two exceeding great uraei which are upon the head of their father Tmu, or (as others say), His two eyes are the two plumes.

'Osiris Ani, the scribe of all the holy offerings, riseth up in his place in triumph; he cometh into his city.'

What then is this? It is the horizon of his father Tmu.

'I have made an end of my shortcomings, and I have put away my faults.'

What then is this? It is the cutting off of the corruptible in the body of Osiris, the scribe Ani, triumphant before all the gods; and all his faults are driven out.

What then is this? It is the purification [of Osiris] on the day of his birth.

'I am purified in my exceeding great double nest which is in Suten henen, on the day of the offerings of the followers of the great god who is therein.'

What then is this? 'Millions of years' is the

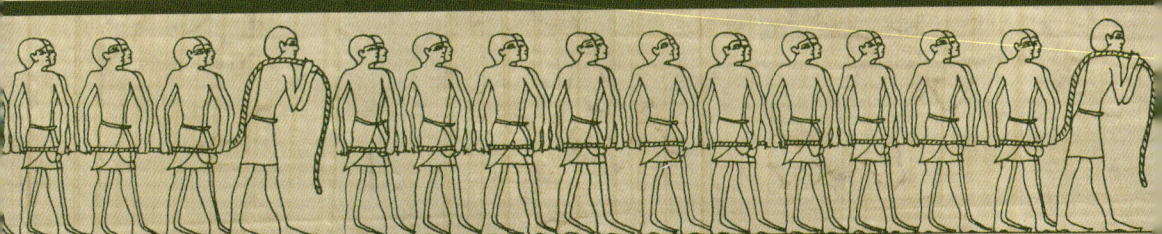

name of the one [nest], 'Green Lake' is the
name of the other; a pool of natron, and a pool
of nitre; or (as others say), 'The Traverser of
Millions of Years' is the name of the one, 'Great
Green Lake' is the name of the other; or (as
others say), 'The Begetter of Millions of Years'
is the name of the one, 'Green Lake' is the name
of the other. Now as concerning the great god
who is in it, it is Ra himself.

'I pass over the way, I know the head[s] of
the Pool of Maata.'

What then is this? It is Re-stau;[54] that is to say,
it is the underworld on the south of Naarut-f,
and it is the northern door of the tomb.

Now as concerning She-Maaat,[55] it is Abtu;
or (as others say), It is the road by which
his father Tmu travelleth when he goeth to
Sekhet-Aaru, which bringeth forth the food
and nourishment of the gods behind the shrine.
Now the Gate of Sert is the gate of the pillars
of Shu, the northern gate of the underworld; or
(as others say), It is the two leaves of the door
through which the god Tmu passeth when he
goeth forth in the eastern horizon of heaven.

'O ye gods who are in the presence [of
Osiris], grant me your arms, for I am the god
who shall come into being among you.'

What then is this? It is the drops of blood
which fell from Ra when he went forth to cut
himself. They sprang into being as the gods
Hu and Sa, who are in the following of Ra and
who accompany Tmu daily and every day.

'I, Osiris, Ani the scribe, triumphant, have filled
up for thee the utchat[56] after it was darkened on
the day of the combat of the Two Fighters.'

What then is this? It is the day on which
Horus fought with Set, who cast filth in the
face of Horus, and when Horus destroyed the
powers of Set. Thoth did this with his own hand.

'I lift the hair[-cloud] when there are
storms in the sky.'

What then is this? It is the right eye of Ra,
which raged against [Set] when he sent it forth.
Thoth raiseth up the hair[-cloud], and bringeth
the eye alive, and whole, and sound, and without
defect to [its] lord; or (as others say), It is the eye
of Ra when it is sick and when it weepeth for its
fellow eye; then Thoth standeth up to cleanse it.

'I behold Ra who was born yesterday from
the buttocks of the cow Meh-urt; his strength is
my strength, and my strength is his strength.'

What then is this? It is the water of heaven,
or (as others say), It is the image of the eye of
Ra in the morning at his daily birth. Meh-urt
is the eye of Ra. Therefore Osiris, the scribe
Ani, triumphant, [is] a great one among the
gods who are in the train of Horus. The words
are spoken for him that loveth his lord.

What then is this? [i.e. who are these gods?]
Mestha, Hapi Tuamautef, and Qebhsennuf.

'Homage to you, O ye lords of right and
truth, and ye holy ones who [stand] behind
Osiris, who utterly do away with sins and
crime, and [ye] who are in the following of the
goddess Hetep-se-khus, grant that I may come
unto you. Destroy ye all the faults which are

within me, even as ye did for the seven Shining Ones who are among the followers of their lord Sepa. Anubis appointed their place on the day [when was said], "Come therefore thither".'

What then is this? These lords of right and truth are Thoth and Astes, lord of Amenta. The holy ones who stand behind Osiris, even Mestha, Hapi, Tuamautef, and Qebhsennuf, are they who are behind the Thigh[57] in the northern sky. They who do away with sins and crime and who are in the following of the goddess Hetep-se-khus are the god Sebek in the waters. The goddess Hetep-se-khus is the eye of Ra, or (as others say), It is the flame which followeth after Osiris to burn up the souls of his foes. As concerning all the faults which are in Osiris, the scribe of the holy offerings of all the gods, Ani, triumphant, [they are all that he hath done against the lords of eternity] since he came forth from his mother's womb. As concerning the seven Shining Ones, even Mestha, Hapi, Tuamautef, Qebhsennuf, Maa-atef-f, Kheri-beq-f, and Horus-Khenti-maa,

Anubis appointed them protectors of the body of Osiris, or (as others say), [set them] behind the place of purification of Osiris; or (as others say), Those seven glorious ones are Netcheh-netcheh, Aqet-qet, An-erta-nef-bes-f-khenti-heh-f,[58] Aq-her-unnut-f,[59] Tesher-maa-ammi-het-Anes,[60] Ubes-hra-per-em-khet khet,[61] and Maa-em-qerh-an-nef-em-hru.[62] The chief of the holy ones who minister in his chamber is Horus, the avenger of his father. As to the day [upon which was said] 'Come therefore thither', it concerneth the words, 'Come then thither', which Ra spake unto Osiris. Lo, may this be decreed for me in Amentet.

'I am the soul which dwelleth in the two tchafi.'

What then is this? It is Osiris [when] he goeth into Tattu and findeth there the soul of Ra; there the one god embraceth the other, and souls spring into being within the two tchafi.[63]

['I am the Cat which fought (?) by the Persea tree hard by in Annu, on the night when the foes of Neb-er-tcher were destroyed.']

What then is this? The male cat is Ra himself,

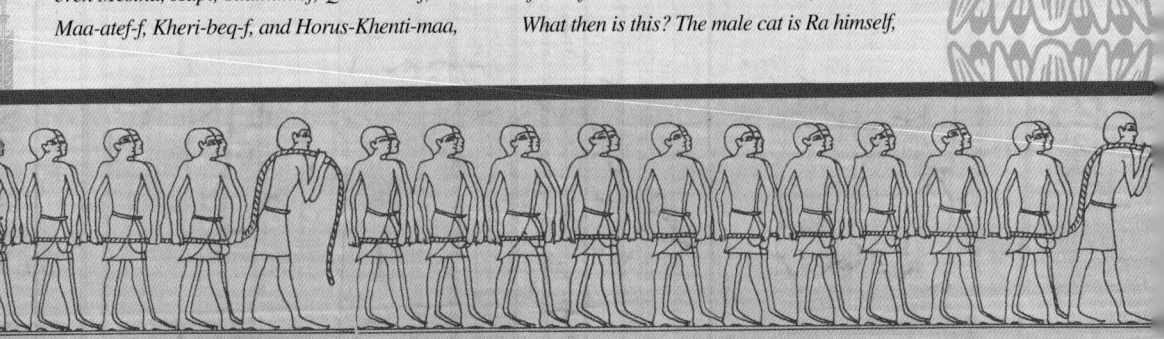

and he is called Maau[64] by reason of the speech of the god Sa [who said] concerning him: 'He is like (maau) unto that which he hath made, and his name became Maau'; or (as others say), It is Shu who maketh over the possessions of Seb to Osiris. As to the fight (?) by the Persea tree hard by, in Annu, it concerneth the children of impotent revolt when justice is wrought on them for what they have done. As to [the words] 'that night of the battle', they concern the inroad [of the children of impotent revolt] into the eastern part of heaven, whereupon there arose a battle in heaven and in all the earth.

'O thou who art in the egg (i.e. Ra), who shinest from thy disk and risest in thy horizon, and dost shine like gold above the sky, like unto whom there is none among the gods, who sailest over the pillars of Shu (i.e. the ether), who givest blasts of fire from thy mouth, [who makest the two lands bright with thy radiance, deliver] the faithful worshippers from the god whose forms are hidden, whose eyebrows are like unto the two arms of the balance on the night of the reckoning of destruction.'

Who then is this? It is An-a-f, the god who bringeth his arm. As concerning [the words] 'that night of the reckoning of destruction,' it is the night of the burning of the damned, and of the overthrow of the wicked at [the sacred] block, and of the slaughter of souls.

Who then is this? It is Nemu, the headsman of Osiris; or (as others say), It is Apep when he riseth up with one head bearing ma'at (i.e. right and truth) [upon it]; or (as others say), It is Horus when he riseth up with two heads, whereof the one beareth ma'at and the other wickedness. He bestoweth wickedness on him that worketh wickedness, and ma'at on him that followeth after righteousness and truth; or (as others say), It is the great Horus who dwelleth in [Se]khem; or (as others say), It is Thoth; or (as others say), It is Nefer-Tmu, [or] Sept, who doth thwart the course of the foes of Neb-er-tcher.

'Deliver me from the Watchers who bear

slaughtering knives, and who have cruel fingers,[65] and who slay those who are in the following of Osiris. May they never overcome me, may I never fall under their knives.'

What then is this? It is Anubis, and it is Horus in the form of Khent-en-maa; or (as others say), It is the Divine Rulers who thwart the works of their [weapons]; it is the chiefs of the sheniu chamber.

'May their knives never get the mastery over me, may I never fall under their instruments of cruelty, for I know their names, and I know the being Matchet[66] who is among them in the house of Osiris, shooting rays of light from [his] eye, but he himself is unseen. He goeth round about heaven robed in the flame of his mouth, commanding Hapi, but remaining himself unseen. May I be strong upon earth before Ra, may I come happily into haven in the presence of Osiris. Let not your offerings be hurtful to me, O ye who preside over your altars, for I am among those who follow after Neb-er-tcher according to the writings of

Khepera. I fly as a hawk, I cackle as a goose; I ever slay, even as the serpent goddess Nehebka.'

What then is this? They who preside at the altars are the similitude of the eye of Ra and the similitude of the eye of Horus.

'O Ra-Tmu, lord of the Great House, prince, life, strength and health of all the gods, deliver thou [me] from the god whose face is like unto that of a dog, whose brows are as those of a man, and who feedeth upon the dead, who watcheth at the Bight of the Fiery Lake, and who devoureth the bodies of the dead and swalloweth hearts, and who shooteth forth filth, but he himself remaineth unseen.' Who then is this? 'Devourer for Millions of Years' is his name, and he dwelleth in the Lake of Unt. As concerning the Fiery Lake, it is that which is in Anrutf, hard by the Shenit chamber. The unclean man who would walk thereover doth fall down among the knives; or (as others say), His name is 'Mathes',[67] and he is the watcher of the door of Amenta; or (as others say), His name is 'Heri-sep-f'.

'Hail, Lord of terror, chief of the lands of the North and South, lord of the red glow, who preparest the slaughter-block, and who dost feed upon the inward parts!'

Who then is this? The guardian of the Bight of Amenta.

What then is this? It is the heart of Osiris, which is the devourer of all slaughtered things. The urerit crown hath been given unto him with swellings of the heart as lord of Suten-henen.

What then is this? He to whom hath been given the urerit crown with swellings of the heart as lord of Suten-henen is Osiris. He was bidden to rule among the gods on the day of the union of earth with earth in the presence of Neb-er-tcher.

What then is this? He that was bidden to rule among the gods is [Horus] the son of Isis, who was appointed to rule in the place of his father Osiris. As to the day of the union of earth with earth, it is the mingling of earth with earth in the coffin of Osiris, the Soul that liveth in Suten-henen, the giver of meat and drink, the destroyer of wrong, and the guide of the everlasting paths.

Who then is this? It is Ra himself.

'Deliver thou [me] from the great god who carrieth away souls, and who devoureth filth and eateth dirt, the guardian of the darkness [who himself liveth] in the light. They who are in misery fear him.'

As concerning the souls within the tchafi [they are those which are] with the god who carrieth away the soul, who eateth hearts, and who feedeth upon offal, the guardian of the darkness who is within the seker boat; they who live in crime fear him.

Who then is this? It is Suti, or (as others say), It is Smam-ur,[68] the soul of Seb.

'Hail, Khepera in thy boat, the twofold company of the gods is thy body. Deliver thou Osiris Ani, triumphant, from the watchers who give judgment, who have been appointed by Neb-er-tcher to protect him and to fasten the fetters on his foes, and who slaughter in the shambles; there is no escape from their grasp. May they never stab me with their knives, may I never fall helpless in their chambers of torture. Never have the things which the gods hate been done by me, for I am pure within the Mesqet. Cakes of saffron have been brought unto him in Tanenet.'

Who then is this? It is Khepera in his boat. It is Ra himself. The watchers who give judgment are the apes Isis and Nephthys. The things which the gods hate are wickedness and falsehood; and he who passeth through the place of purification within the Mesqet is Anubis, who is behind the chest which holdeth the inward parts of Osiris.

He to whom saffron cakes have been brought in Tanenet is Osiris; or (as others say), The saffron cakes in Tanenet are heaven and earth, or (as others say), They are Shu, strengthener of the two lands in Suten-henen.

The saffron cakes are the eye of Horus; and Tanenet is the grave of Osiris.

Tmu hath built thy house, and the two-fold Lion-god hath founded thy habitation; lo! drugs are brought, and Horus purifieth and Set strengtheneth, and Set purifieth and Horus strengtheneth.

'The Osiris, the scribe Ani, triumphant before Osiris, hath come into the land, and hath possessed it with his feet. He is Tmu, and he is in the city.'

'Turn thou back, O Rehu, whose mouth shineth, whose head moveth, turn thou back from before his strength'; or (as others say), Turn thou back from him who keepeth watch and is unseen. 'The Osiris Ani is safely guarded. He is Isis, and he is found with [her] hair spread over him. I shake it out over his brow. He was conceived in Isis and begotten in Nephthys; and they cut off from him the things which should be cut off.'

Fear followeth after thee, terror is upon thine arms. Thou art embraced for millions of years in the arms [of the nations]; mortals go round about thee. Thou smitest down the mediators of thy foes, and thou seizest the arms of the powers of darkness. The two sisters (i.e. Isis and Nephthys) are given to thee for thy delight. Thou hast created that which is in Kheraba, and that which is in Annu. Every god feareth thee, for thou art exceeding great and terrible; thou [avengest] every god on the man that curseth him, and thou shootest out arrows…Thou livest according to thy will; thou art Uatchit, the Lady of Flame. Evil cometh among those who set themselves up against thee.

What then is this? The hidden in form, granted of Menhu, is the name of the tomb. He seeth [what is] in [his] hand is the name of the shrine, or (as others say), the name of the block. Now he whose mouth shineth and whose head moveth is a limb of Osiris, or (as others say), of Ra. Thou spreadest thy hair and I shake it out over his brow is spoken concerning Isis, who hideth in her hair and draweth her hair over her. Uatchi, the Lady of Flames, is the eye of Ra.

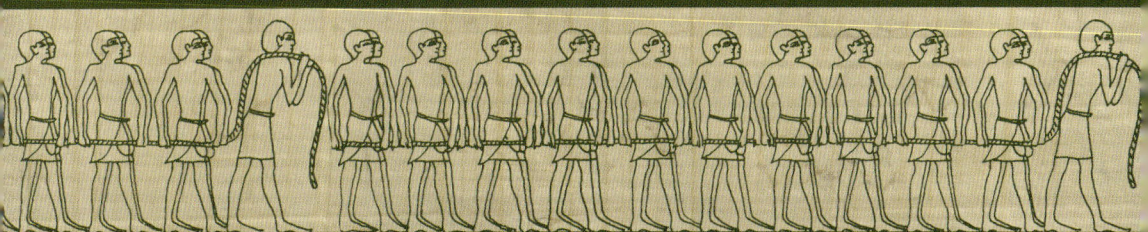

PLATES 11–12

In the upper line of Plates 11 and 12 there is a series of seven Arits, or mansions, through which the deceased is supposed to pass. In the lower line are the ten *Sebkhets*, or pylon-shaped gateways.

FIRST PYLON

1. Ani and his wife Thuthu approaching the first Arit,[69] the cornice of which is ornamented with emblems of power, life, and stability. At the entrance sit three gods, the first having the head of a hare, the second the head of a serpent, and the third the head of a crocodile. The first holds an ear of corn (?), and each of the others a knife.

THE FIRST ARIT. *The name of the doorkeeper is Sekhet-hra-asht-aru;*[70] *the name of the watcher is Meti-heh; the name of the herald is Ha-kheru.*[71]

[WORDS TO BE SPOKEN WHEN OSIRIS COMETH TO THE FIRST ARIT IN AMENTA.] *Saith Ani, triumphant, when he cometh to the first Arit: 'I am the mighty one who createth his own light. I have come unto thee, O Osiris, and, purified from that which defileth thee, I adore thee. Lead on; name not the name of*

FIRST ARIT   SECOND ARIT   THIRD ARIT   FOURTH ARIT

SECOND PYLON   THIRD PYLON   FOURTH PYLON   FIFTH PYLON   SIXTH PYLON

Re-stau unto me. Homage to thee, O Osiris, in thy might and in thy strength in Re-stau. Rise up and conquer, O Osiris, in Abtu. Thou goest round about heaven, thou sailest in the presence of Ra, thou seest all the beings who have knowledge. Hail Ra, who circlest in [the sky]. Verily I say [unto thee], O Osiris, I am a godlike ruler. Let me not be driven hence[72] nor from the wall of burning coals. [I have] opened the way in Re-stau; I have eased the pain of Osiris; [I have] embraced that which the balance I hath weighed; [I have] made a path for him in the great valley, and [he] maketh a path. Osiris shineth(?).'

2. The second Arit, guarded by three gods, the first with the head of a lion, the second the head of a man, and the third the head of a dog. Each one holds a knife. THE SECOND ARIT. *The name of the doorkeeper is Un-hat; the name of the watcher is Seqet-hra; the name of the herald is Uset.*

Saith Osiris Ani when he cometh unto this Arit: 'He sitteth to do his heart's desire, and he weigheth words as the second of Thoth. The strength of Thoth humbleth the hidden Maata gods who feed upon Maat throughout the years [of their lives]. I make offerings at the moment when [he] passeth on his way; I pass on and enter on the way; Grant thou that I may pass through and that I may gain sight of Ra together with those who make offerings.'

3. The third Arit, guarded by three gods, the first with the head of a jackal, the second the head of a dog, and the third the head of a serpent. The first holds an ear of corn (?), and each of the others a knife. THE THIRD ARIT. *The name of the doorkeeper is Qeq-hauau-ent-pehui;*[73] *the name of the watcher is Se-res-hra;*[74] *the name of the herald is Aaa.*[75]

Saith Osiris Ani [when he cometh to this Arit]: 'I am hidden [in] the great deep, [I am] the judge of the Rehui.[76] *I have come and I have done away with the offences of Osiris. I am building up the standing place which cometh forth from his* urerit *(?) crown. I have done his business in Abtu, I have opened the way in Re-stau, I have eased the pain which was in Osiris. I have made straight his standing place, and I have made [his] path. He shineth in Re-stau.'*

4. The fourth Arit, guarded by three gods, the first with the head of a man, the second the head of a hawk, and the third the head of a lion. The first holds an ear of corn and each of the others a knife. THE FOURTH ARIT. *The name of the doorkeeper is Khesef-hra-asht-kheru;[77] the name of the watcher is Seres-tepu; the name of the herald is Khesef-At.[78]*

Saith Osiris, the scribe Ani, triumphant [when he cometh to this Arit]: 'I am the [mighty] bull, the son of the ancestress of Osiris. O grant ye that his father, the lord of his godlike companions, may bear witness for him. Here the guilty are weighed in judgment. I have brought unto his nostrils eternal life. I am the son of Osiris, I have made the way, I have passed thereover into Neter-khert.'

5. The fifth Arit, guarded by three gods, the first with the head of a hawk, the second the head of a man, and the third the head of a snake. Each holds a knife. THE FIFTH ARIT. *The name of the doorkeeper is Ankh-f-em-fent;[79] the name of the watcher is Shabu; the name of the herald is Teb-hra-keha-kheft.*

Saith Osiris, the scribe Ani, triumphant [when he cometh to this Arit]: 'I have brought unto thee the bones of thy jaws in Re-stau, I have brought thee thy backbone in Annu, gathering together all thy members there. I have driven back Apep for thee. I have poured water upon the wounds; I have made a path among you. I am the Ancient One among the gods. I have made the offering of Osiris, who hath triumphed with victory, gathering his bones and bringing together all his limbs.'

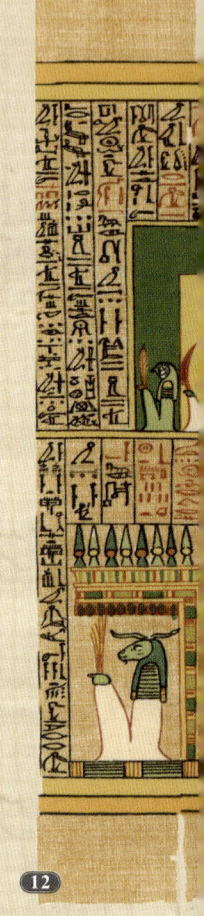

6. The sixth Arit, guarded by three gods, the first with the head of a jackal, and the second and third the head of a dog. The first holds an ear of corn (?), and each of the others a knife.

THE SIXTH ARIT. *The name of the doorkeeper is Atek-au-kehaq-kheru; the name of the watcher is An-hri; the name of the herald is Ates-hra.*

Saith Osiris, the scribe Ani [when he cometh to this Arit]: 'I have come daily, I have come daily. I have made the way; I have passed along that which was created by Anubis. I am the lord of the urerit *crown… magical words. I, the avenger of right and truth, have avenged his eye. I have swathed the eye of Osiris, [I have] made the way]; Osiris Ani hath passed along [it] with you…'*

7. The seventh Arit, guarded by three gods, the first with the head of a hare, the second the head of a lion, and the third the head of a man. The first and second hold a knife, and the third an ear of corn (?).

THE SEVENTH ARIT. *The name of the doorkeeper is Sekhem-Matenu-sen; the name of the watcher is Aa-maa-kheru, and the name of the herald is Khesef-khemi.*

Saith Osiris, [the scribe] Ani [when he cometh to this Arit]: 'I have come unto thee, O Osiris, who art cleansed of [thine] impurities. Thou goest round about heaven, thou seest Ra, thou seest the beings who have knowledge. Hail Only One! Behold, thou art in the sektet *boat, He goeth round the horizon of heaven. I speak what I will unto his body; it waxeth strong and it cometh to life, as he spake. Thou turnest back his face. Prosper thou for me all the ways [which lead] unto thee!'*

SEVENTH PYLON

SIXTH ARIT   SEVENTH ARIT

H PYLON   NINTH PYLON   TENTH PYLON

PLATES 11–12, LOWER REGISTER SHOWING THE PYLONS

1. Ani and his wife Thuthu, with hands raised in adoration, approaching the first *Sebkhet* or Pylon, which is guarded by a bird-headed deity wearing a disk on his head and sitting in a shrine, the cornice of which is decorated with *khakeru*[80] ornaments.

Words to be spoken when [Ani] cometh unto the first Pylon. *Saith Osiris Ani, triumphant: 'Lo, the lady of terrors, with lofty walls, the sovereign lady, the mistress of destruction, who uttereth the words which drive back the destroyers, who delivereth from destruction him that travelleth along the way. The name of the doorkeeper is Neruit.'*

2. The second Pylon, which is guarded by a lion-headed deity seated in a shrine, upon the top of which is a serpent.

Words to be spoken when [Ani] cometh unto the second Pylon. *Saith Osiris, the scribe Ani, triumphant: 'Lo, the lady of heaven, the mistress of the world, who devoureth with fire, the lady of mortals; how much greater is she than all men! The name of the doorkeeper is Mes-Ptah.'*

3. The third Pylon, which is guarded by a man-headed deity seated in a shrine, the upper part of which is ornamented with the two *utchats* and the emblems of the orbit of the sun and of water.

Words to be spoken when [Ani] cometh unto the third Pylon of the house of Osiris. *Saith the scribe Ani, triumphant: 'Lo, the lady of the altar, the mighty one to whom offerings are made, the beloved (?) of every god, who saileth up to Abtu. The name of the doorkeeper is Sebaq.'*

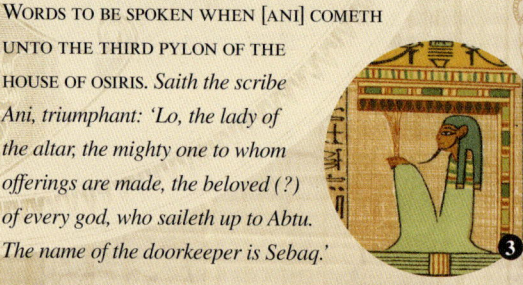

4. The fourth Pylon, which is guarded by a cow-headed deity seated in a shrine, the cornice of which is ornamented with uraei wearing disks.

Words to be spoken when [Ani] cometh unto the fourth pylon. *Saith Osiris, the scribe Ani, [triumphant]: 'Lo, she who prevaileth with knives, mistress of the world, destroyer of the foes of the Still-Heart, she who decreeth the escape of the needy from evil hap. The name of the doorkeeper is Nekau.'*

5. The fifth Pylon, which is guarded by the hippopotamus deity, with her fore-feet resting upon the buckle, the emblem of protection, seated in a shrine, the cornice of which is ornamented with [symbols] emblematic of flames of fire.

Words to be spoken when [Ani] cometh unto the fifth pylon. *Saith Osiris, the scribe Ani, triumphant: 'Lo, the flame, the lady of breath (?) for the nostrils; one may not advance to entreat her shall not come into her presence. The name of the doorkeeper is Hentet-Arqiu.'*

6. The sixth Pylon, which is guarded by a deity in the form of a man holding a knife and a besom[81] and seated in a shrine, above which is a serpent.

WORDS TO BE SPOKEN WHEN [ANI] COMETH UNTO THE SIXTH PYLON. *Saith Osiris, the scribe Ani, triumphant: 'Lo, the lady of light, the mighty one, to whom men cry aloud; man knoweth neither her breadth nor her height; there was never found her like from the beginning (?). There is a serpent thereover whose size is not known; it was born in the presence of the Still-Heart. The name of the doorkeeper is Semati.'*

7. The seventh Pylon, which is guarded by a ram-headed deity holding a besom and seated in a shrine, the cornice of which is decorated with *khakeru* ornaments.

WORDS TO BE SPOKEN WHEN [ANI] COMETH UNTO THE SEVENTH PYLON. *Saith Osiris, the scribe Ani, triumphant: 'Lo, the robe which doth clothe the feeble one (i.e. the deceased), weeping for what it loveth and shroudeth. The name of the doorkeeper is Sakti-f.'*

8. The eighth Pylon, which is guarded by a hawk wearing the crowns of the North and South, seated on a sepulchral chest with closed doors; before him is a besom, and behind him is the *utchat*. Above the shrine are two human-headed hawks, emblems of the souls of Ra and Osiris, and two emblems of life.

WORDS TO BE SPOKEN WHEN [ANI] COMETH UNTO THE EIGHTH PYLON. *Saith Osiris, the scribe Ani, triumphant: 'Lo, the blazing fire, the*

*flame whereof cannot be quenched, with
tongues of flame which reach afar, the
slaughtering one, the irresistible, through
which one may not pass by reason of the hurt
which it doeth. The name of the doorkeeper is
Khu-tchet-f.'* [82]

9. The ninth Pylon, which is guarded by
a lion-headed deity wearing a disk and
holding a besom, seated in a shrine, the
cornice of which is ornamented with
uraei wearing disks.

WORDS TO BE SPOKEN WHEN [ANI]
COMETH UNTO THE NINTH PYLON. *Saith
Osiris Ani, triumphant: 'Lo, she who is
chiefest, the lady of strength, who giveth quiet
of heart to her lord. Her girth is three hundred
and fifty measures; she is clothed with mother-
of-emerald of the South; and she raiseth up the
godlike form and clotheth the feeble one… The
name of the doorkeeper is Ari-su-tchesef.'* [83]

10. The tenth Pylon, which is guarded by a
ram-headed deity wearing the *atef* crown
and holding a besom, seated in a shrine,
upon the top of which are two serpents.

WORDS TO BE SPOKEN WHEN [ANI]
COMETH UNTO THE TENTH PYLON. *Saith
Osiris Ani, [triumphant]: 'Lo, she who is
loud of voice, she who causeth those to
cry who entreat her, the fearful one who
terrifieth, who feareth none that are therein.
The name of the doorkeeper is Sekhen-ur.'*

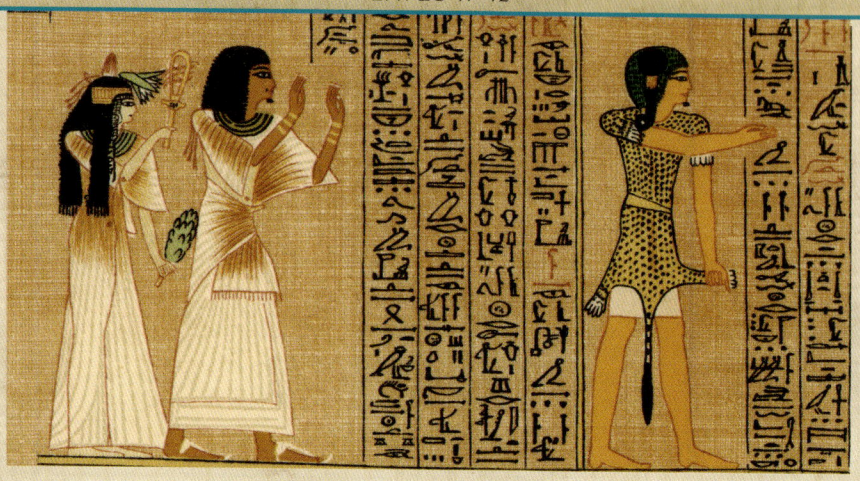

Plate 12 upper register:[84] The priest An-maut-f,[85] who has on the right side of his head the lock of Heru-pa-khrat, or Horus the Child, and who wears a leopard's skin, introducing Ani and his wife to the gods whose names are given in Plates 13 and 14.

An-maut-f saith: 'I have come unto you, O mighty and godlike rulers who are in heaven and in earth and under the earth; and I have brought unto you Osiris Ani. He hath not sinned against any of the gods. Grant ye that he may be with you for all time.'

The adoration of Osiris, lord of Re-stau, and of the great company of the gods who are in the netherworld beside Osiris, the scribe Ani, who saith: 'Homage to thee, O ruler of Amenta, Unnefer within Abtu! I have come unto thee, and my heart holdeth right and truth. There is no sin in my body, nor have I lied wilfully, nor have I done aught with a false heart. Grant thou to me food in the tomb, and that I may come into [thy] presence at the altar of the lords of right and truth, and that I may enter into and come forth from the netherworld (my soul not being turned back), and that I may behold the face of the Sun, and that I may behold the Moon for ever and ever.'

Plate 12 lower register: The priest Se-mer-f, who has on the right side of his head the lock of Heru-pa-khrat and wears a leopard's skin, introducing Ani and his wife to the gods whose names are given in Plates 13 and 14.

Se-mer-f saith: 'I have come unto you, O godlike rulers who are in Re-stau, and I have brought unto you Osiris Ani. Grant ye [to him], as to the followers of Horus, cakes and water, and air, and a homestead in Sekhet-Hetep.' [86]

The adoration of Osiris, the lord of everlastingness, and of all the godlike rulers of Re-stau, by Osiris, [the scribe Ani], who saith: 'Homage to thee, O king of Amenta, prince of Akert, I have come unto thee. I know thy ways, I am furnished with the forms which thou takest in the underworld. Grant thou to me a place in the underworld near unto the lords of right and truth. May my homestead be abiding in Sekhet-hetep, and may I receive cakes in thy presence.'

PLATE 13

Upper register: A pylon, or gateway, surmounted by the feathers of Maat and uraei wearing disks. Lower register: A pylon, surmounted by Anubis and an *utchat*.

['*Hail Thoth, who madest Osiris victorious over his enemies, make thou Osiris [the scribe Ani] to be victorious over his enemies, as thou didst make Osiris victorious over his enemies, in the presence of the godlike rulers who are with Ra and Osiris in Annu, on the night of 'the things for the night',[87] and on the night of battle, and on the shackling of the fiends, and on the day of the destruction of Neb-er-tcher.'*][88]

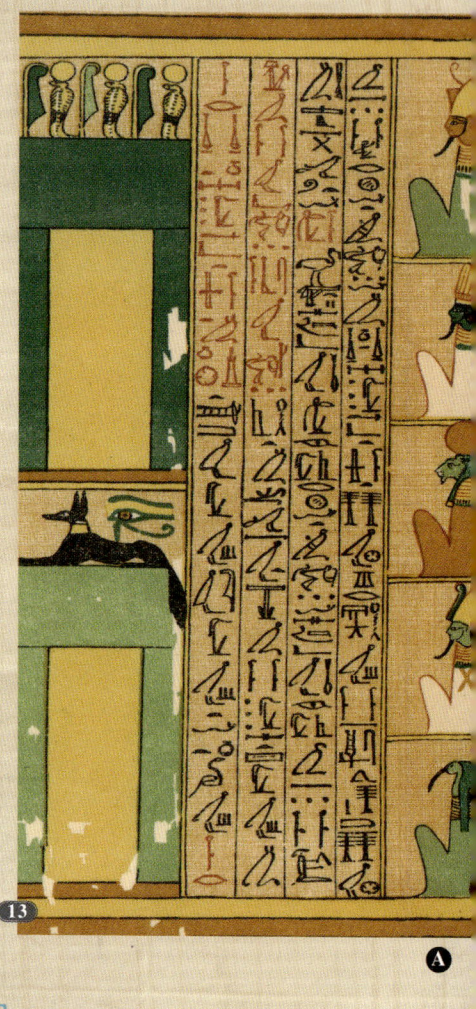

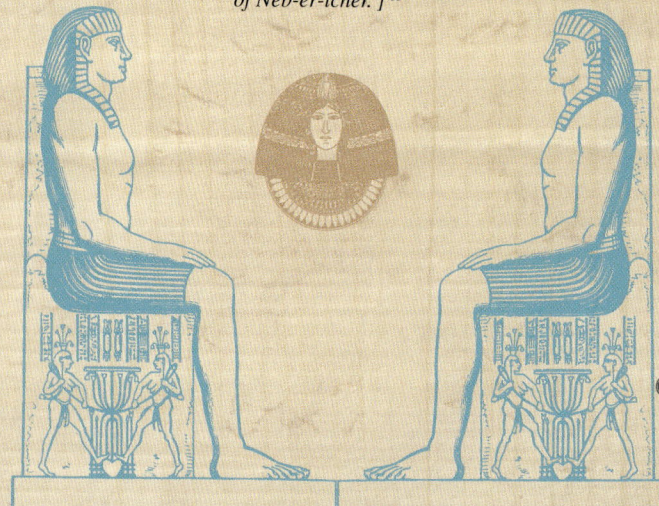

PLATE 13 57

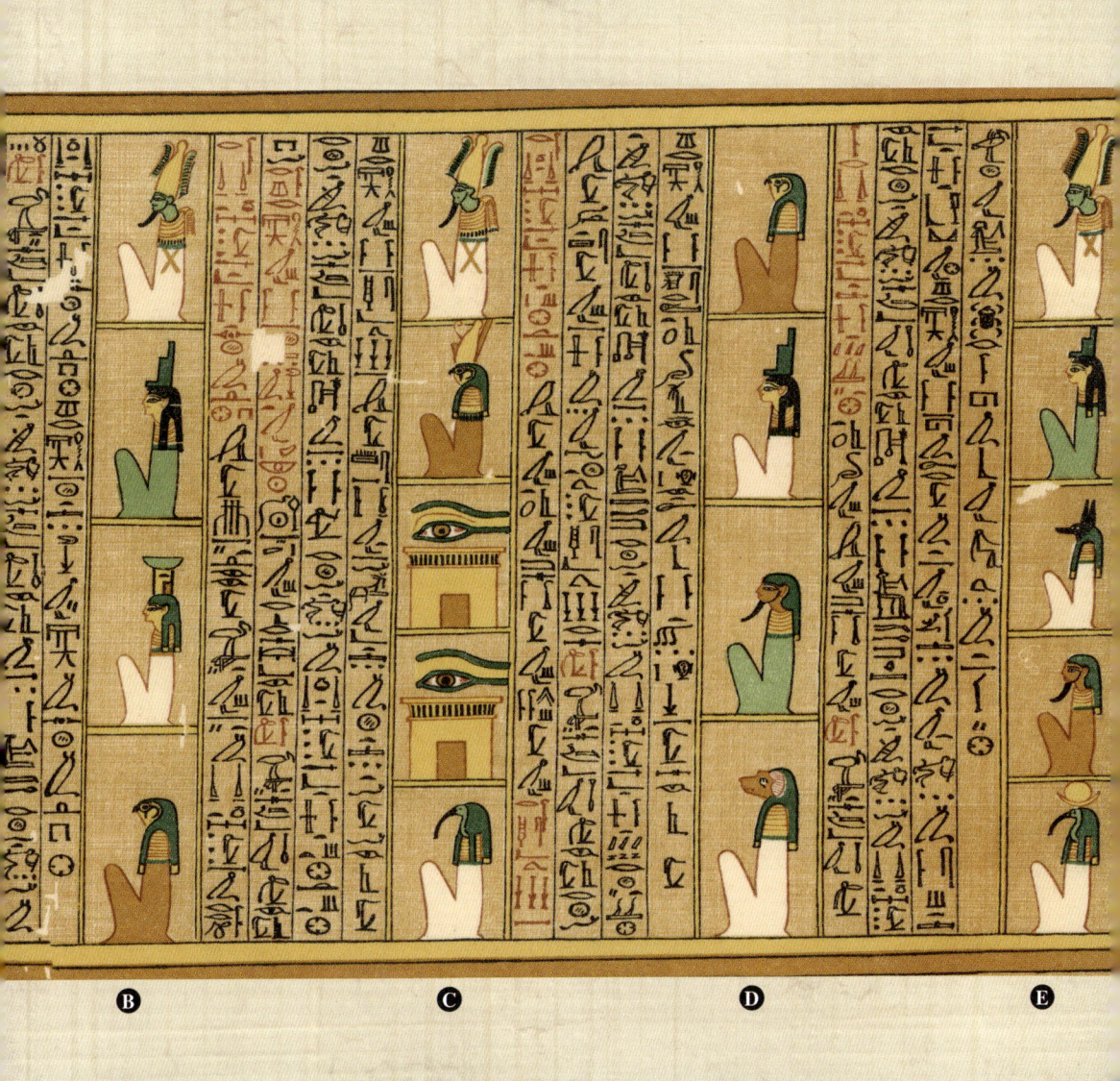

B   C   D   E

A. The gods Tmu, Shu, Tefnut, Osiris, and Thoth.

The great godlike rulers in Annu are Tmu, Shu, Tefnut, [Osiris, and Thoth], and the shackling of the Sebau signifieth the destruction of the fiends of Set when he worketh evil a second time.

'Hail, Thoth, who madest Osiris victorious over his enemies, make thou the Osiris Ani to be victorious over his enemies in the presence of the great divine beings who are in Tattu, on the night of making the Tat to stand up in Tattu.'

B. The gods Osiris, Isis, Nephthys, and Horus.

The great godlike rulers in Tattu are Osiris, Isis, Nephthys, and Horus, the avenger of his father. Now the 'night of making the Tat to stand up in Tattu' signifieth [the lifting up of] the arm and shoulder of Osiris, lord of Sekhem; and these gods stand behind Osiris [to protect him] even as the swathings which clothe him.

'Hail, Thoth, who madest Osiris victorious over his enemies, make thou the Osiris Ani triumphant over his enemies in the presence of the great godlike rulers who are in Sekhem, on the night of the things of the night [festival] in Sekhem.'

C. The gods Osiris and Horus, two *utchats* upon pylons, and the god Thoth.

The great godlike rulers who are in Sekhem are Horus, who is without sight, and Thoth, who is with the godlike rulers in Naarerutf. Now the 'night of the things of the night festival in Sekhem' signifieth the light of the rising sun on the coffin of Osiris.

'Hail, Thoth, who madest Osiris victorious over his enemies, make thou the Osiris Ani triumphant over his enemies in the presence of the great godlike rulers in Pe and Tep, on the night of setting up the columns of Horus, and of making him to be established the heir of the things which belonged to his father.'

PLATE 13 59

D. The gods Horus, Isis, Mestha, and Hapi.
The great divine rulers who are in Pe and Tep are Horus, Isis, Mestha, and Hapi. Now setting up the columns of Horus [signifieth] the command given by Set unto his followers: 'Set up columns upon it.'

'Hail, Thoth, who madest Osiris victorious over his enemies, make thou the Osiris-Ani triumphant over his enemies in the presence of the great godlike rulers in...Rekhit, on the night when Isis lay down to keep watch in order to make lamentation for her brother Osiris.'

E. The gods [Osiris], Isis, Anubis, Mestha, and Thoth.
The great godlike rulers who are in...Rekhit are Isis, Horus (?), and Mestha.

'Hail, Thoth, who madest Osiris victorious over his enemies, make thou the Osiris, the scribe Ani (triumphant in peace!), to be victorious over his enemies in the presence of the great godlike ones who are in Abtu, on the night of the god Naker, at the separation of the wicked dead, at the judgment of spirits made just, and at the arising of joy in Tenu.'

PLATE 14

F. The gods Osiris, Isis, and Ap-uat, and the Tet.

The great godlike rulers who are in Abtu are Osiris, Isis, and Ap-uat.

'Hail, Thoth, who madest Osiris victorious over his enemies, make thou the Osiris Ani, the scribe and teller of the sacred offerings of all the gods, to be victorious over his enemies in the presence of the godlike rulers who judge the dead, on the night of the condemnation of those who are to be blotted out.'

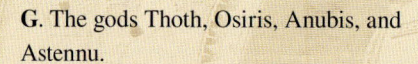

G. The gods Thoth, Osiris, Anubis, and Astennu.

The great godlike rulers in the judgment of the dead are Thoth, Osiris, Anubis, and Astennu. Now the 'condemnation of those who are to be blotted out' is the withholding of that which is so needful to the souls of the children of impotent revolt.

'Hail, Thoth, who madest Osiris victorious over his enemies, make thou the Osiris, the scribe Ani (triumphant!), to be victorious over his enemies in the presence of the great godlike rulers, on the festival of the breaking and turning up of the earth in Tattu, on the night of the breaking and turning up of the earth in their blood and of making Osiris to be victorious over his enemies.'

H. The three gods of the festival of breaking up the earth in Tattu.

When the fiends of Set come and change themselves into beasts, the great godlike rulers, on the festival of the breaking and turning up of the earth in Tattu, slay them in the presence of the gods therein, and their blood floweth among them as they are smitten down. These things are allowed to be done by them by the judgment of those who are in Tattu.

'Hail, Thoth, who madest Osiris victorious over his enemies, make thou the Osiris Ani to be victorious over his enemies in the presence of the godlike rulers who are in Naarutef, on the night of him who concealeth himself in divers forms, even Osiris.'

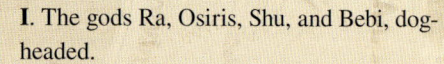

I. The gods Ra, Osiris, Shu, and Bebi, dog-headed.

The great godlike rulers who are in Naarutef are Ra, Osiris, Shu, and Bebi. Now the 'night of him who concealeth himself in divers forms, even Osiris', is when the thigh [and the head], and the heel, and the leg, are brought nigh unto the coffin of Osiris Un-nefer.

'Hail, Thoth, who madest Osiris victorious over his enemies, make thou the Osiris Ani (triumphant before Osiris) victorious over his enemies in the presence of the great godlike rulers who are in Re-stau, on the night when Anubis lay with his arms and his hands over the things behind Osiris, and when Horus was made to triumph over his enemies.'

PLATE 14   61

14

F   G   H   I   J

J. The gods Horus, Osiris, Isis, and…(?)
*The great godlike rulers in Re-stau are
Horus, Osiris, and Isis. The heart of Osiris
rejoiceth, and the heart of Horus is glad; and
therefore are the East and the West at peace.*

'*Hail Thoth, who madest Osiris victorious
over his enemies, make thou the Osiris Ani,
the scribe and teller of the divine offerings
of all the gods, to triumph over his enemies
in the presence of the ten companies of great
godlike rulers who are with Ra and with
Osiris and with every god and goddess in the
presence of Neb-er-tcher. He hath destroyed
his enemies, and he hath destroyed every evil
thing belonging unto him.*'

Rubric: *This chapter being recited, the
deceased shall come forth by day, purified after
death, and [he shall make all] the forms (or
transformations) which his heart shall dictate.
Now if this chapter be recited over him, he shall
come forth upon earth, he shall escape from
every fire; and none of the foul things which
appertain unto him shall encompass him for
everlasting and for ever and for ever.*

PLATE 15

A seated statue of Ani, the scribe, upon which the ceremony of 'opening the mouth', is being performed by the *Sem* priest, clad in a panther's skin and holding in his right hand the instrument *Ur heka*, i.e. 'mighty one of enchantments'. In front of the statue are: the sepulchral chest; the instruments Seb-ur, Tun-tet, and Temanu and the object Pesh-en-kef.

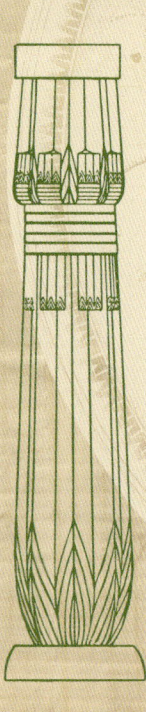

THE CHAPTER OF OPENING THE MOUTH OF OSIRIS, THE SCRIBE ANI.

To be said: *'May Ptah open my mouth, and may the god of my town loose the swathings, even the swathings which are over my mouth. Moreover, may Thoth, being filled and furnished with charms, come and loose the bandages, the bandages of Set which fetter my mouth; and may the god Tmu hurl them at those who would fetter [me] with them, and drive them back. May my mouth be opened, may my mouth be unclosed by Shu with his iron[89] knife, wherewith he opened the mouth of the gods. I am Sekhet, and I sit upon the great western side of heaven. I am the great goddess Sah among the souls of Annu. Now as concerning every charm and all the words which may be spoken against me, may the gods resist them, and may each and every one of the company of the gods withstand them.'*

THE CHAPTER OF BRINGING CHARMS UNTO OSIRIS ANI [IN NETER-KHERT]. *[He saith]:* '*I am Tmu-Khepera, who gave birth unto himself upon the thigh of his divine mother. Those who are in Nu*[90] *are made wolves, and those who are among the godlike rulers are become hyenas. Behold, I gather together the charm from every place where it is and from every man with whom it is, swifter than greyhounds and fleeter than light. Hail thou who towest along the* makhent *boat of Ra, the stays of thy sails and of thy rudder are taut in the wind as thou sailest over the Lake of Fire in Neter-khert. Behold, thou gatherest together the charm from every place where it is and from every man with whom it is, swifter than greyhounds and fleeter than light, [the charm] which createth the forms of existence from the mother's thigh (?) and createth the gods from (or in) silence, and which giveth the heat of life unto the gods. Behold, the charm is given unto me from wheresoever it is [and from him with whom it is], swifter than greyhounds and fleeter than light,' or, (as others say), 'fleeter than a shadow'.*

The scribe Ani, clothed in white, and with his heart in his right hand, addressing the god Anubis. Between them is a necklace of several rows of coloured beads, the clasp of which is in the shape of a pylon or gateway, and to which is attached a pectoral bearing a representation

PLATE 15
63

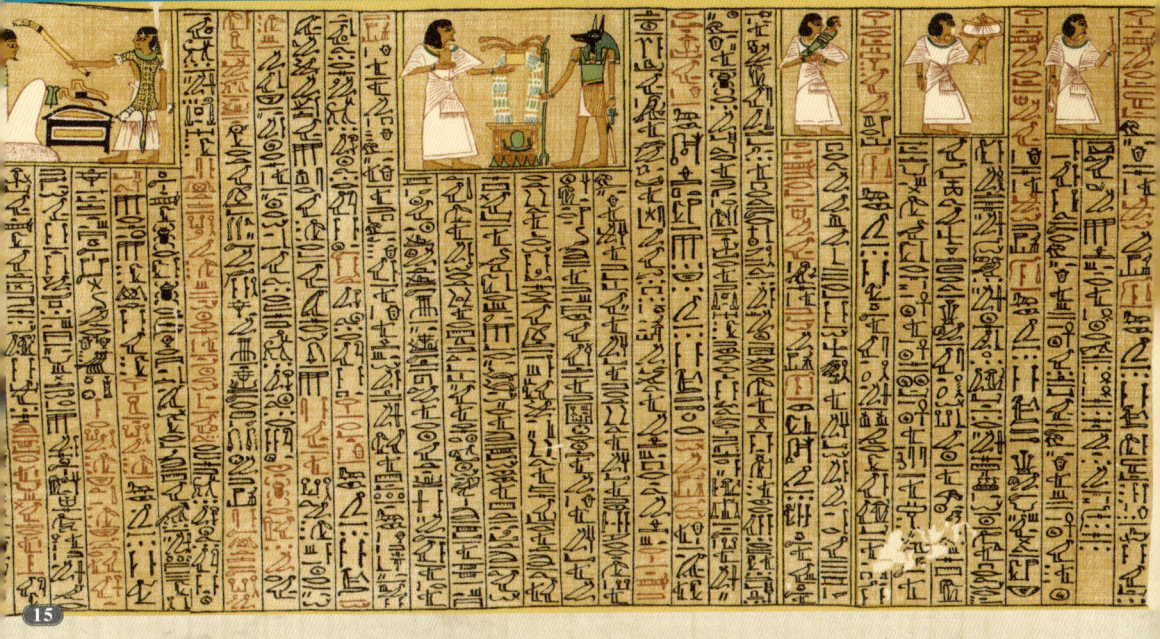

of the boat of the Sun, wherein is set a scarab, emblematic of the Sun.

CHAPTER OF GIVING A HEART UNTO OSIRIS ANI IN THE UNDERWORLD. *[Ani saith]: 'May my heart be with me in the House of Hearts.*[91] *May my heart be with me, and may it rest in [me], or I shall not eat of the cakes of Osiris on the eastern side of the Lake of Flowers, [neither shall I have] a boat wherein to go down the Nile, and another wherein to go up, nor shall I go forward in the boat with thee. May my mouth be given unto me that I may speak with it, and my two feet to it walk withal, and my two hands and arms to overthrow my foe. May the doors of heaven be opened unto me; may Seb, the Prince of the gods,* open wide his two jaws unto me; may he open my two eyes which are blinded; may he cause me to stretch out my feet which are bound together; and may Anubis make my legs firm that I may stand upon them. May the goddess Sekhet make me to rise so that I may ascend unto heaven, and there may that be done which I command in the House of the Ka of Ptah.*[92] *I know my heart, I have gotten the mastery over my heart, I have gotten the mastery over my two hands and arms, I have gotten the mastery over my feet, and I have gained the power to do whatsoever my ka pleaseth. My soul shall not be shut off from my body at the gates of the underworld; but I shall enter in peace, and I shall come forth in peace.'*

THE CHAPTER OF NOT LETTING THE HEART OF OSIRIS, THE SCRIBE OF THE SACRED OFFERINGS OF ALL THE GODS, ANI, TRIUMPHANT, BE DRIVEN FROM HIM IN THE UNDERWORLD. *Ani saith: 'My heart, my mother; my heart, my mother. My heart whereby I come into being. May there be nothing to withstand me at [my] judgment; may there be no resistance against me by the Tchatcha; may there be no parting of thee from me in the presence of him who keepeth the Scales! Thou art my* ka *within my body, [which] knitteth and strengtheneth my limbs. Mayest thou come forth in the place of happiness [to which] I advance. May the* Shenit,[93] *who make men to stand fast, not cause my name to stink.'*[94]

Ani holding his soul in the form of a human-headed bird.

CHAPTER OF NOT LETTING THE SOUL OF A MAN BE TAKEN AWAY FROM HIM IN THE UNDERWORLD. *Osiris the scribe Ani saith: 'I, even I, am he who came forth from the water-flood which I make to overflow and which becometh mighty as the River [Nile].'*

Ani carrying a sail, emblematic of breath and air.

CHAPTER OF GIVING BREATH IN THE UNDERWORLD. *Saith Osiris Ani: 'I am the Egg of the Great Cackler, and I watch and guard that great place which the god Seb hath proclaimed upon earth. I live; and it liveth; I grow strong, I live, I sniff the air. I am Utcha-aab, and I go round behind [to protect] his egg. I have thwarted the chance of Set, the mighty one of strength. Hail thou who makest pleasant the world with* tchefa *food, and who dwellest in the blue [sky]; watch over the babe in his cot when he cometh forth unto thee.'*

Ani standing, with a staff in his left hand.

THE CHAPTER OF NOT LETTING THE HEART OF A MAN BE TAKEN AWAY FROM HIM IN THE UNDERWORLD. *Saith Osiris Ani, triumphant: 'Turn thou back, O messenger of all the gods. Is it that thou art come to carry away this my heart which liveth? My heart which liveth shall not be given unto thee. [As I] advance, the gods give ear unto my supplications, and they fall down upon their faces wheresoever they be.'*

PLATE 16

Ani standing, with both hands raised in prayer, before four gods who are seated on a pedestal in the form of Maat; before him is his heart set upon a pedestal.

THE CHAPTER OF NOT LETTING THE HEART OF A MAN BE TAKEN AWAY FROM HIM IN THE UNDERWORLD. *Saith Osiris Ani: 'Hail, ye who carry away hearts, [hail] ye who steal hearts! Ye have done. Homage to you, O ye lords of eternity, ye possessors of everlastingness, take ye not away this heart of Osiris Ani in your* grasp, *this heart of Osiris. And cause ye not evil words to spring up against it; because this heart of Osiris Ani is the heart of the one of many names, the mighty one whose words are his limbs, and who sendeth forth his heart to dwell in his body. The heart of Osiris Ani is pleasant unto the gods; he is victorious, he hath*

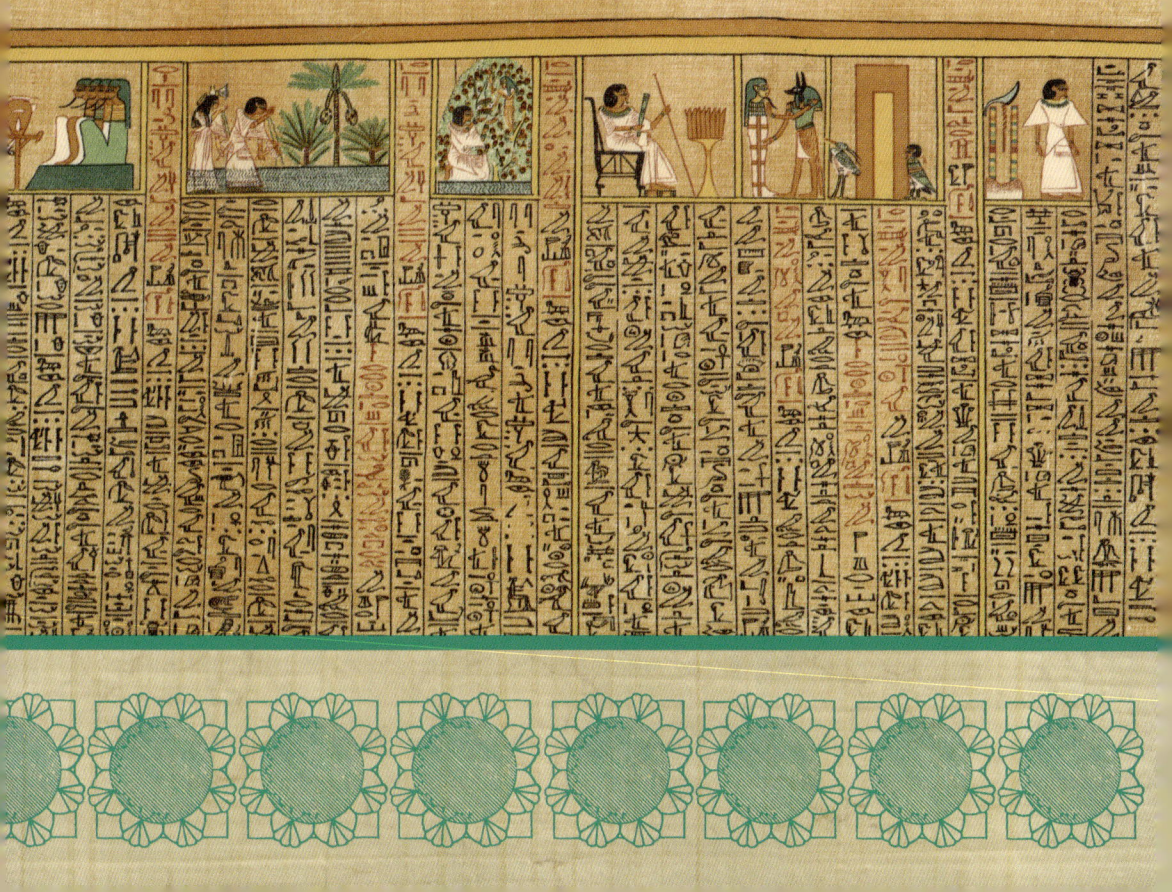

gotten power over it; he hath not revealed what hath been done unto it. He hath gotten power over his own limbs. His heart obeyeth him, he is the lord thereof, it is in his body, and it shall never fall away therefrom. I, Osiris, the scribe Ani, victorious in peace, and triumphant in the beautiful Amenta and on the mountain of eternity, bid thee be obedient unto me in the underworld.'

Ani and his wife Thuthu, each holding the emblem of air in the left hand, and drinking water with the right from a pool, on the borders of which are palm trees laden with fruit.

THE CHAPTER OF BREATHING THE AIR AND OF HAVING POWER OVER THE WATER IN THE UNDERWORLD. *Saith Osiris Ani: 'Open to me! Who art thou then, and whither dost thou fare? I am one of you. Who is it with thee? It is Merti. Separate thou from him, each from each, when thou enterest the Mesqen. He letteth me sail to the temple of the divine beings who have found their faces(?). The name of the boat is "Assembler of Souls"; the name of the oars is "Making the hair to stand on end"; the name of the hold is "Good"; and the name of the rudder is "Making straight for the middle"...*[95]*...Grant ye to me vessels of milk together with cakes, loaves of bread, cups of drink, and flesh in the temple of Anubis.'*

   Rubric: If this chapter be known [by Ani] he shall go in after having come forth from the underworld.

Ani kneeling beside a pool of water, where grows a sycamore tree; in the tree appears the goddess Nut pouring water into Ani's hands from a vessel.

THE CHAPTER OF SNIFFING THE AIR, AND OF GETTING POWER OVER THE WATERS IN THE UNDERWORLD. *Saith Osiris Ani: 'Hail, sycamore tree of the goddess Nut! Grant thou to me of the water and the air which are in thee. I embrace thy throne which is in Unnu, and I watch and guard the egg of the Great Cackler. It groweth, I grow; it liveth, I live; it sniffeth the air, I sniff the air, I the Osiris Ani, in triumph.'*

Ani seated upon a chair before a table of offerings; in his right hand he holds the *kherp* sceptre and in his left a staff.

THE CHAPTER OF NOT DYING A SECOND TIME IN THE UNDERWORLD. *Saith Osiris Ani: 'My place of hiding is opened, my place of hiding is revealed! Light hath shone in the darkness. The eye of Horus hath ordered my coming into being, and the god Apuat hath nursed me. I have hidden myself with you, O ye stars that never set. My brow is like unto that of Ra; my face is open; my heart is upon its throne; I utter words, and I know; in very truth, I am Ra himself. I am not treated with scorn, and violence is not done unto me. Thy father, the son of Nut, liveth for thee. I am thy first-born, and I see thy mysteries. I am crowned like unto the king of the gods, and I shall not die a second time in the underworld.'*

PLATE 16 67

The mummy of Ani embraced by Anubis, the god of the dead.

THE CHAPTER OF NOT CORRUPTING IN THE UNDERWORLD. *Saith Osiris Ani: 'O thou who art without motion like unto Osiris! O thou who art without motion like unto Osiris! O thou whose limbs are without motion like unto [those of] Osiris! Let not thy limbs be without motion, let them not corrupt, let them not pass away, let them not decay; let it be done unto me even as if I were the god Osiris.'*

Rubric: If this chapter be known by the Osiris Ani, he shall not corrupt in the underworld.

A doorway. By one post stands the soul of Ani in the form of a human-headed hawk and by the other the [*bennu*?] bird.

THE CHAPTER OF NOT PERISHING AND OF BECOMING ALIVE IN THE UNDERWORLD. *Saith Osiris Ani: 'Hail, children of Shu! Hail, children of Shu, [children of] the place of the dawn, who as the children of light have gained possession of his crown. May I rise up and may I fare forth like Osiris.'*

Ani the scribe standing with his back to a block and knife.

THE CHAPTER OF NOT ENTERING IN UNTO THE BLOCK. *Saith Osiris Ani: 'The four bones of my neck and of my back are joined together for me in heaven by Ra, the guardian of the earth. This was granted on the day when my rising up out of weakness upon my two feet was ordered, on the day when the hair was cut off. The bones of my neck and of my back have been joined together by Set and by the company of the gods, even as they were in the time that is past; may nothing happen to break them apart. Make ye [me] strong against my father's murderer. I have gotten power over the two earths. Nut hath joined together my bones, and [I] behold [them] as they were in the time that is past [and I] see [them] even in the same order as they were [when] the gods had not come into being in visible forms. I am Penti, I, Osiris the scribe Ani, triumphant, am the heir of the great gods.'*

PLATE 17

Ani standing in adoration before three gods, each of whom holds a sceptre in his left hand, and the symbol of life in his right.

THE CHAPTER OF NOT LETTING A MAN PASS OVER TO THE EAST IN THE UNDERWORLD. *Saith Osiris Ani: 'Hail, manhood of Ra, which advanceth and beateth down opposition; things which have been without movement for millions of years come into being through the god Baba. Hereby am I made stronger than the strong, and hereby have I more power than they who are mighty. And therefore neither shall I be borne away nor carried by force to the East, to take part in the festivals of the fiends; nor shall there [be given unto me] cruel gashes with knives, nor shall I be shut in on every side, nor gored by the horns [of the god Khepera]...'* [96]

Ani adoring a god in a boat whose head is turned face backwards.

ANOTHER CHAPTER.[97] *[Saith Osiris Ani]: 'So then shall no evil things be done unto me by the fiends, neither shall I be gored by the horns [of Khepera]; and the manhood of Ra, which is the head of Osiris, shall not*

be swallowed up. Behold me, I enter into my homestead, and I reap the harvest. The gods speak with me. Gore thou not them, O Ra-khepera. In very truth sickness shall not arise in the eye of Tmu nor shall it be destroyed. Let me be brought to an end, may I not be carried into the East to take part in the festivals of the fiends who are my enemies; may no cruel gashes be made in me. I, Osiris, the scribe Ani, the teller of the divine offerings of all the gods, triumphant with happy victory, the lord to be revered, am not carried away into the East.'

THE CHAPTER OF NOT LETTING THE HEAD OF A MAN BE CUT OFF FROM HIM IN THE UNDERWORLD. *Saith Osiris Ani: 'I am the great One, son of the great One; I am Fire, the son of Fire, to whom was given his head after it had been cut off. The head of Osiris was not carried away from him; let not the head of Osiris Ani be carried away from him. I have knit together my bones, I have made myself whole and sound; I have become young once more; I am Osiris, the Lord of eternity.'*

PLATE 17   69

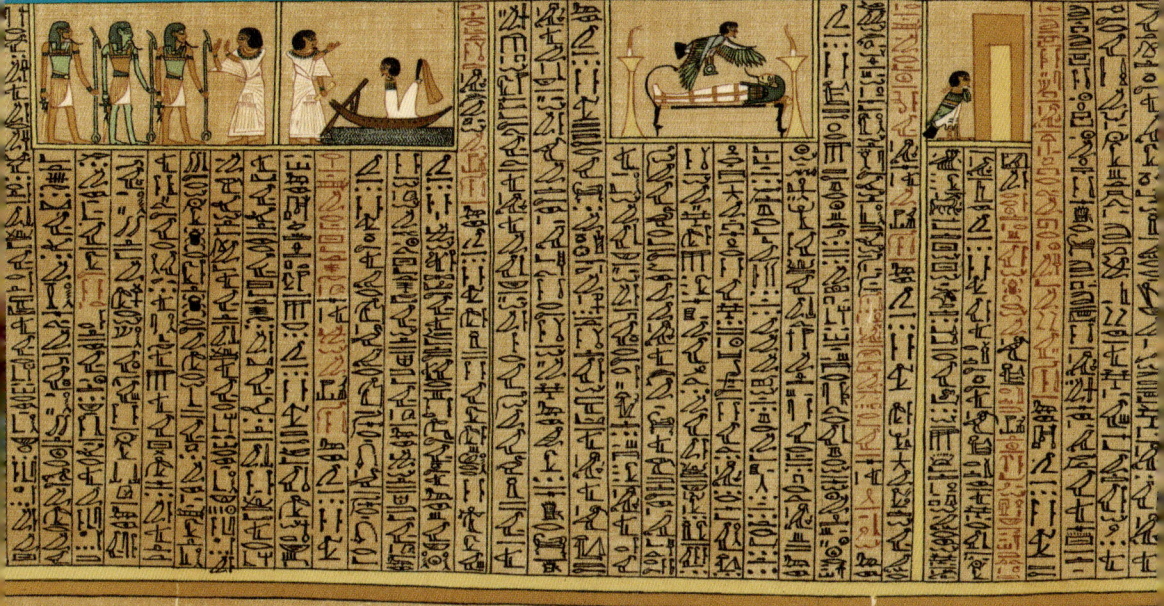

The mummy of Ani lying on a bier; above is his soul in the form of a human-headed bird, holding *shen*, the emblem of eternity, in its claws. At the head and foot stands an incense burner with fire in it. THE CHAPTER OF CAUSING THE SOUL TO BE UNITED TO ITS BODY IN THE UNDERWORLD. *Saith Osiris Ani: 'Hail, thou god Annitu! Hail, O Runner, dwelling in thy hall! O thou great god, grant thou that my soul may come unto me from wheresoever it may be. If it would tarry, then bring thou unto me my soul from wheresoever it may be. [If] thou findest [me], O eye of Horus, make thou me to stand up like those beings who are like unto Osiris and who never lie down in death. Let not Osiris Ani, triumphant, triumphant, lie down in death in Annu, the land wherein souls are joined unto their bodies, even in thousands. My soul doth bear away with it my victorious spirit whithersoever it goeth… If it would tarry, grant thou that my soul may look upon my body. [If] thou findest [me], O eye of Horus, make thou me to stand up like unto those…*[98]

Hail, ye gods, who row in the boat of the Lord of Millions of Years, who tow it above the underworld, who make it to pass over the ways of Nu, who make souls to enter into their glorified bodies, whose hands are filled with righteousness, and whose fingers grasp your sceptres, destroy ye the foe. The boat of the Sun rejoiceth, and the great god advanceth in peace. Behold [ye gods], grant that this soul of Osiris Ani may come forth triumphant before the gods, and triumphant before you, from the eastern horizon of heaven, to follow unto the place where it was yesterday, in peace, in peace, in Amenta. May he behold his body, may he rest in his glorified frame, may he never perish, and may his body never see corruption.'

    Rubric: *To be said over a golden [figure of a] soul inlaid with precious stones, which is to be placed on the neck of Osiris.*

Ani's soul, in the form of a human-headed bird, standing in front of a pylon.

THE CHAPTER OF NOT LETTING THE SOUL OF A MAN BE CAPTIVE IN THE UNDERWORLD.

Saith Osiris Ani: 'Hail thou who art exalted, thou who art adored, thou mighty one of souls, thou Ram (or Soul), possessor of terrible power, who dost put fear of thee into the hearts of the gods, thou who art crowned upon thy mighty throne! It is he who maketh the path for the khu *and for the soul of Osiris Ani. I am furnished [with that which I need], I am a* khu *furnished [with that which I need], I have made my way unto the place wherein are Ra and Hathor.'*

    Rubric: *If this chapter be known, Ani shall become like unto a shining being fully equipped in the underworld. He shall not be stopped at any door in the underworld from going in and coming out millions of times.*

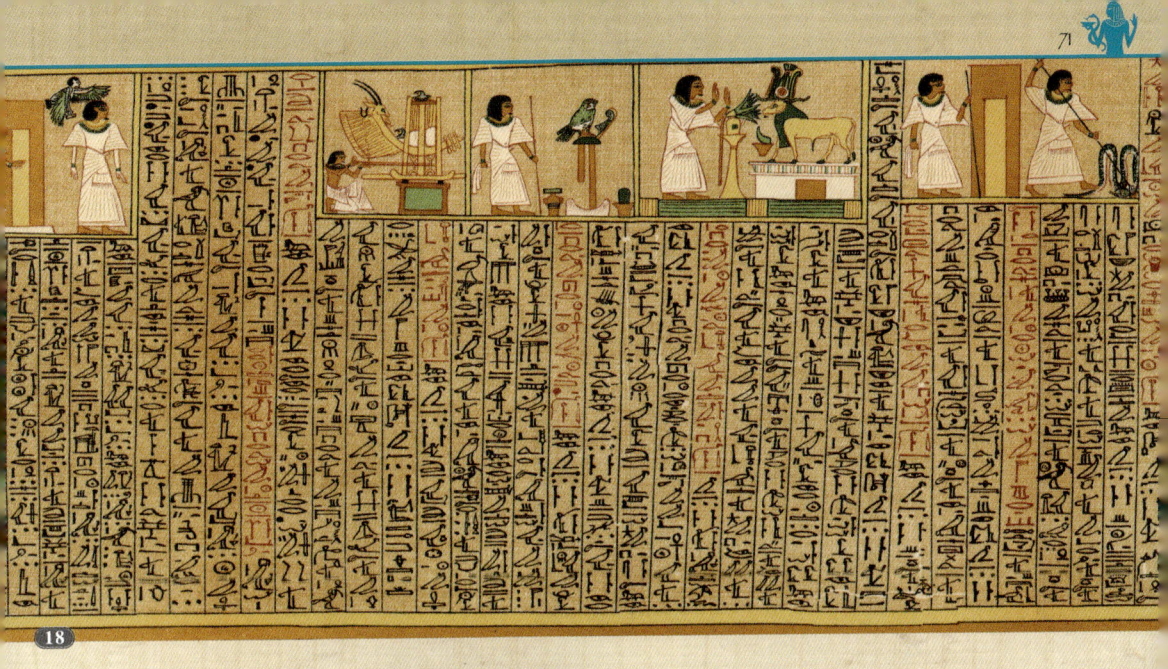

18

PLATE 18

Ani standing at the doorway of the tomb; and Ani's shadow, accompanied by his soul.

THE CHAPTER OF OPENING THE TOMB TO THE SOUL OF THE SHADOW, OF COMING FORTH BY DAY, AND OF GETTING POWER OVER THE LEGS. *Saith Osiris, the scribe Ani, triumphant: 'The place of bondage is opened, that which was shut is opened, and the place of bondage is opened unto my soul [according to the bidding of] the eye of Horus. I have bound and stablished glories upon the brow of Ra. [My] steps are made long, [my] thighs are lifted up; I have passed along the great path, and my limbs are strong. I am Horus, the avenger of his father, and*

I bring the ureret *crown to rest upon its place. The path of souls is opened [to my soul]. My soul seeth the great god within the boat of Ra on the day of souls. My soul is in the front among those who tell the years. Come; the eye of Horus, which stablisheth glories upon the brow of Ra and rays of light upon the faces of those who are with the limbs of Osiris, hath delivered my soul. O shut ye not in my soul, fetter ye not my shade; may it behold the great god within the shrine on the day of the judgment of souls, may it repeat the words of Osiris. May those beings whose dwelling-places are hidden, who fetter the limbs of Osiris, who fetter the souls of the* khu, *who shut in the shade[s] of the dead and can do evil unto me – may they do no evil unto me, may they turn away their path from me. Thy heart is with thee; may my soul and my* khu *be prepared against their attack. May I sit down among the great rulers who dwell in their abodes; may my soul not be set in bondage by those who fetter the limbs of Osiris, and who fetter souls, and who shut in the shade[s] of the dead. The place which thou possessest, is it not Heaven?'*

Rubric: *If this chapter be known, he shall come forth by day and his soul shall not be shut in.*

Ani kneeling, with both hands raised in adoration, by the side of the Seker[99] boat placed upon its sledge.

THE CHAPTER OF WALKING WITH THE TWO LEGS, AND OF COMING FORTH UPON EARTH. *Saith Osiris Ani: 'Thou hast done all thy work, O Seker, thou hast done all thy work, O Seker, in thy dwelling place within my legs in the underworld. I shine above the Leg[100] of the Sky, I come forth from heaven; I recline with the glorified spirits. Alas! I am weak and feeble; alas! I am weak and feeble. I walk. I am weak and feeble in the presence of those who gnash with the teeth in the underworld, I Osiris, the scribe Ani, triumphant in peace.'*

The emblem of Amenta and Ani standing with a staff in his left hand.

THE CHAPTER OF PASSING THROUGH AMENTA, AND OF COMING FORTH BY DAY. *Saith Osiris Ani: 'The hour (?) openeth; the head of Thoth is sealed up; perfect is the eye of Horus. I have delivered the eye of Horus which shineth with splendours on the forehead of Ra, the father of the gods. I am the same Osiris, dwelling in Amenta. Osiris knoweth his day and that he shall not live therein; nor shall I live therein. I am the Moon among the gods; I shall not come to an end. Stand up, therefore, O Horus; Osiris hath counted thee among the gods.'*

THE CHAPTER OF COMING FORTH BY DAY, AND OF LIVING AFTER DEATH. *Saith*

PLATE 18 73

Osiris Ani: 'Hail, Only One, shining from the Moon! Hail, Only One, shining from the Moon! Grant that this Osiris Ani may come forth among the multitudes which are round about thee; let him be established as a dweller among the shining ones; and let the underworld be opened unto him. And behold Osiris, Osiris Ani shall come forth by day to do his will upon earth among the living.'

Ani, standing with both hands raised in adoration before a ram crowned with plumes and disk; in front of the ram is a table, upon which are a libation vase and a lotus flower.

THE CHAPTER OF COMING FORTH BY DAY, HAVING PASSED THROUGH THE TOMB. *Saith Osiris Ani: 'Hail Soul, thou mighty one of strength! Verily I am here, I have come, I behold thee. I have passed through the underworld, I have seen [my] father Osiris, I have scattered the gloom of night. I am his beloved one. I have come; I behold my father Osiris. I have stabbed Set to the heart. I have done the things [needed] by my father Osiris. I have opened every way in heaven and upon earth. I am the son beloved of his father Osiris. I have become a ruler, I have become glorious, I am furnished [with what I need]. Hail, all ye gods, and all ye shining ones, make ye a way for me, the Osiris, the scribe Ani, triumphant.'*

Ani, with a staff in his left hand, standing before a door.

THE CHAPTER OF MAKING A MAN TO RETURN TO SEE AGAIN HIS HOME UPON EARTH. *Saith Osiris Ani: 'I am the Lion-god coming forth with strides. I have shot forth arrows, I have wounded [the prey], I have wounded the prey. I am the eye of Horus; I have opened the eye of Horus in his hour. I am come unto the furrows. Let Osiris Ani come in peace.'*

Ani piercing a serpent.

ANOTHER CHAPTER OF ONE WHO COMETH FORTH BY DAY AGAINST HIS FOES IN THE UNDERWORLD. *Saith Osiris Ani: 'I have divided the heavens, I have passed through the horizon, I have traversed the earth, [following] upon his footsteps. I am borne away by the mighty and shining ones because, behold, I am furnished with millions of years which have magic virtues. I eat with my mouth, I chew with my jaws; and, behold, I am the god who is the lord of the underworld: May there be given unto me, Osiris Ani, that which abideth for ever without corruption.'*

PLATE 19

Ani standing, with both hands raised in adoration, before Ra, hawk-headed and seated in a boat floating upon the sky. On the bows sits Heru-pa-khrat (Harpocrates), or 'Horus the child'; and the side is ornamented with the feathers of Maat, and the *utchat*. The handles of the oars and the tops of the rowlocks are shaped as hawks' heads, and on the blades of the oars are two *utchat*.

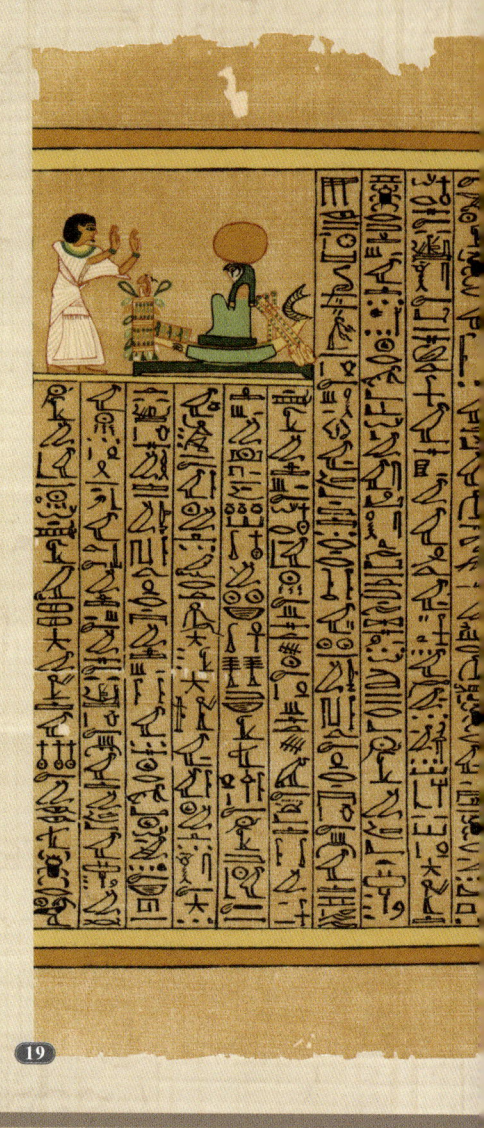

A HYMN OF PRAISE TO RA WHEN HE RISETH UPON THE HORIZON, AND WHEN HE SETTETH IN THE [LAND OF] LIFE. *Saith Osiris, the scribe Ani: 'Homage to thee, O Ra, when thou risest [as] Tmu-Heru-khuti (Harmachis), Thou art adored [by me] when thy beauties are before mine eyes, and when thy shining rays [fall] upon my body. Thou goest forth in peace in the* sektet *boat with [fair] winds, and thy heart is glad; [thou goest forth] in the* atet *boat, and its heart is glad. Thou stridest over the heavens in peace, and thy foes are cast down; the never-resting stars sing hymns of praise unto thee, and the stars which never set glorify thee as thou sinkest in the horizon of Manu, O thou who art beautiful in the two parts of heaven, thou lord who livest and art established, O my lord! Homage to thee, O*

19

PLATE 19   75

thou who art Ra when thou risest, and Tmu when thou settest in beauty. Thou risest and shinest upon the back of thy mother [the sky], O thou who art crowned king of the gods. Nut doth homage unto thee, and everlasting and never-changing order embraceth thee at morn and at eve. Thou stridest over the heaven, being glad of heart, and the Lake Testes is at peace. The Fiend hath fallen to the ground; his arms and his hands have been hewn off, and the knife hath severed the joints of his body. Ra hath a fair wind; the sektet boat goeth forth and sailing along it cometh into port. The gods of the South and of the North, of the West and of the East praise thee, from whom all forms of life came into being. Thou sendest forth the word, and the earth is flooded with silence, O thou only One, who livedst in heaven before ever the earth and the mountains were made. O Runner, Lord, only One, thou maker of things which are, thou hast moulded the tongue of the company of the gods, thou hast drawn forth whatsoever cometh from the waters, and thou springest up from them over the flooded land of the Lake of Horus. Make me to sniff the air which cometh forth from thy nostrils, and the north wind which cometh forth from thy mother [the Sky]. Make thou glorious my shining form, O Osiris, make thou strong my soul. Thou art worshipped in peace, O lord of the gods, thou art exalted by reason of thy wondrous works. Shine with thy rays of light upon my body day by day, upon me, Osiris, the scribe, the teller of the divine offerings of all the gods, the overseer of the granary of the lords of Abydos, the royal scribe in truth, who loveth him (i.e., Ra); Ani, triumphant in peace.'

PLATE 19   77

Ani, standing with both hands raised in adoration. Behind him is his wife.

A HYMN OF PRAISE. 'O OSIRIS, *lord of eternity, Un-nefer, Horus of the two horizons, whose forms are manifold, whose creations are without number, Ptah-Seker-Tem in Annu, the lord of the tomb, and the creator of Memphis and of the gods, the guide of the underworld, whom [the gods] glorify when thou settest in Nut. Isis embraceth thee in peace, and she driveth away the fiends from the mouth of thy paths. Thou turnest thy face upon Amenta, thou makest the world to shine as with* smu *metal. The dead rise up to behold thee, they breathe the air and they look upon thy face when the disk shineth on its horizon; their hearts are at peace for that they behold thee, O thou who art eternity and everlastingness.'*

'Homage to thee, [O lord of] starry deities in An, and of heavenly beings in Kher-aba; thou god Unti, who art more glorious than the gods who are hidden in Annu.

Homage to thee, O An in Antes (?), Horus, thou dweller in both horizons, with long strides thou stridest over heaven, O thou who dwellest in both horizons.

Homage to thee, O soul of everlastingness, thou Soul who dwellest in Tattu, Un-nefer, son of Nut; thou art lord of Akert.

Homage to thee in thy dominion over Tattu; the urerit *crown is established upon thy head; thou art the one whose strength is in himself, and thou dwellest in peace in Tattu.*

Homage to thee, O lord of the acacia tree, the seker *boat is set upon its sledge; thou turnest back the Fiend, the worker of evil, and thou causest the* utchat *to rest upon its seat.*

Homage to thee, O thou who art mighty in thine hour, thou great and mighty god, dweller in An-rut-f, lord of eternity and creator of everlastingness; thou art the lord of Suten-henen.

Homage to thee, O thou who restest upon Right and Truth, thou art the lord of Abtu, and thy limbs are joined unto Ta-sertet; thou art he to whom fraud and guile are hateful.

Homage to thee, O thou who art within thy boat, thou bringest Hapi [i.e., the Nile] forth from his source; the light shineth upon thy body, and thou art the dweller in Nekhen.

Homage to thee, O creator of the gods, thou King of the North and of the South; O Osiris, victorious, ruler of the world in thy gracious seasons; thou art the lord of the world.

O grant thou unto me a path whereon I may pass in peace, for I am just and true; I have not spoken lies wittingly, nor have I done aught with deceit.'

PLATE 20

siris and Isis in a sepulchral shrine.

A HYMN OF PRAISE TO RA WHEN HE RISETH IN THE EASTERN PART OF THE HEAVEN. *They who are in his train rejoice, and lo! Osiris Ani in triumph saith 'Hail, thou Disk, thou lord of rays, who risest in the horizon day by day. Shine thou with thy beams of light upon the face of Osiris Ani, who is victorious: for he singeth hymns of praise unto thee at dawn, and he maketh thee to set at eventide with words of adoration. May the soul of Osiris Ani, the triumphant one, come forth with thee from heaven, may he go forth in the* atet *boat, may he come into port in the* sektet *boat, may he cleave his path among the never-resting stars in the heavens.'*

Osiris Ani, being at peace and in triumph, adoreth his lord, the lord of eternity, saying: 'Homage to thee, O Horus of the two horizons, who art Khepera the self-created; when thou risest on the horizon and sheddest thy beams of light upon the lands of the North and the South thou art beautiful, yea beautiful, and all the gods rejoice when they behold thee, the King of heaven. The goddess Nebt-Unnet is stablished upon thy head; her portions of the South and of the North are upon thy brow; she taketh her place before thee. The god Thoth is stablished in the bows of thy boat to destroy utterly all thy foes. Those who dwell in the underworld come forth to meet thee, bowing in homage as they come towards thee, and to behold [thy] beautiful image. And I have come before thee that I may be with thee to behold thy Disk every day. May I not be shut in the tomb, may I not be turned back, may the limbs of my body be made new again when I view thy beauties, even as do all thy favoured ones, because I am one of those who worshipped thee whilst they lived upon earth. May I come in unto the land of eternity, may I come even unto the everlasting land, for behold, O my lord, this hast thou ordained for me.'

And lo, Osiris Ani, triumphant in peace, the triumphant one, saith 'Homage to thee, O thou who risest in thy horizon as Ra, thou art stablished by a law which changeth not nor can it be altered. Thou passest over the sky, and every face watcheth thee and thy course, for thou hast been hidden from their gaze. Thou dost show thyself at dawn and at eventide day by day. The sektet *boat, wherein is thy majesty, goeth forth with might; thy beams shine upon [all] faces; [the number] of thy yellow rays cannot be known, nor can thy bright beams be told. The lands of the gods, and the colours of the eastern lands of Punt, must be seen, ere that which is hidden [in thee] may be measured [by man].*

PLATE 20 79

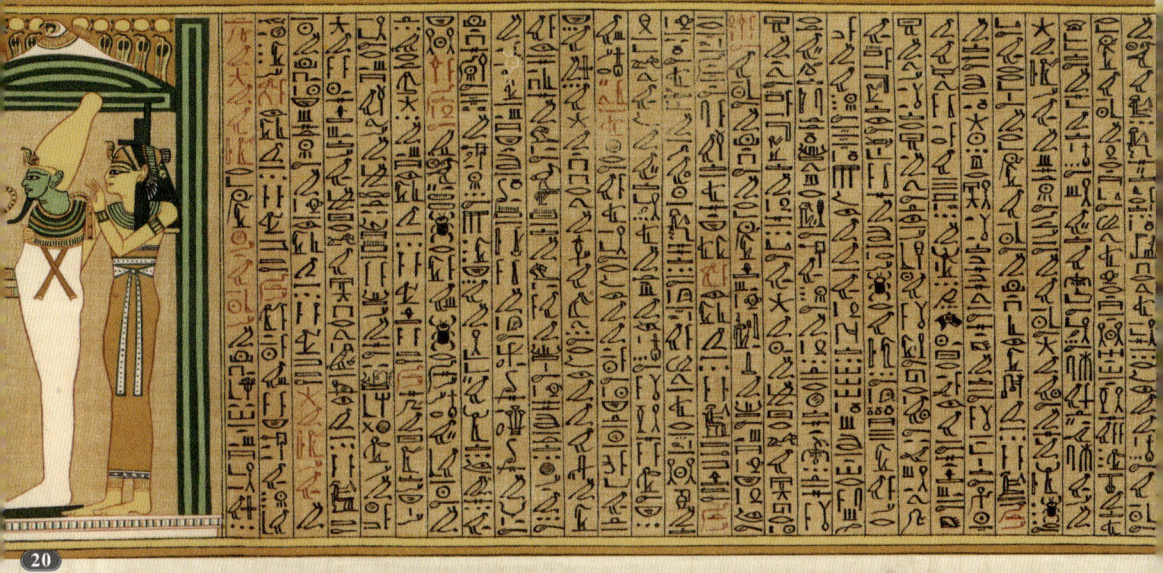

20

Alone and by thyself thou dost manifest thyself [when] thou comest into being above Nu. May Ani advance, even as thou dost advance; may he never cease [to go forward], even as thy majesty ceaseth not [to go forward], even though it be for a moment; for with strides dost thou in one little moment pass over the spaces which would need hundreds of thousands and millions of years [for man to pass over; this] thou doest, and then dost thou sink down. Thou puttest an end to the hours of the night, and thou dost number them, even thou; thou endest them in thine own appointed season, and the earth becometh light. Thou settest thyself before thy handiwork in the likeness of Ra; thou risest in the horizon.'

Osiris, the scribe Ani, triumphant, declareth his praise of thee when thou shinest, and when thou risest at dawn he crieth in his joy at thy birth: 'Thou art crowned with the majesty of thy beauties; thou mouldest thy limbs as thou dost advance, and thou bringest them forth without birth-pangs in the form of Ra, as thou dost climb up into the upper air. Grant thou that I may come unto the heaven which is everlasting, and unto the mountain [where dwell] thy favoured ones. May I be joined unto those shining beings, holy and perfect, who are in the underworld; and may I come forth with them to behold thy beauties when thou shinest at eventide and goest to thy mother Nut. [Ed. Text continues on next plate.]

PLATE 21

Thou dost place thy disk in the West, and my two hands are [raised] in adoration [of thee] when thou settest as a living being. Behold, thou art the maker of eternity, and thou art adored [when] thou settest in the heavens. I have given my heart unto thee without wavering, O thou who art mightier than the gods.'

Osiris Ani, triumphant, saith: 'A hymn of praise to thee, O thou who risest like unto gold, and who dost flood the world with light on the day of thy birth. Thy mother giveth thee birth upon [her] hand, and thou dost give light unto the course of the Disk. O thou mighty Light, who shinest in the heavens, thou dost strengthen the generations of men with the Nile-flood, and dost cause gladness in all lands, and in all cities, and in all the temples. Thou art glorious by reason of thy splendours, and thou makest strong thy ka with hu and tchefau foods. O thou who art the mighty one of victories, thou who art the Power of [all] Powers, who dost make strong thy throne against the powers of wickedness, who art glorious in majesty in the sektet boat, and who art exceeding mighty in the atet boat, make thou glorious Osiris Ani with victory in the netherworld; grant thou that in the underworld he may be void of sin. I pray thee to put away [his] faults behind thee; grant that he may be one of thy venerable servants who are with the shining ones; may he

be joined unto the souls which are in Ta-sertet; and may he journey into the Sekhet-Aaru by a prosperous and happy path, he the Osiris, the scribe Ani, triumphant.

Thou shalt come forth into heaven, thou shalt pass over the sky, thou shalt be joined unto the starry deities. Praises shall be offered unto thee in thy boat, thou shalt be hymned in the atet boat, thou shalt behold Ra within his shrine, thou shalt set together with his disk day by day, thou shalt see the ant fish when it springeth into being in the waters of turquoise, and thou shalt see the abtu fish in his hour. May it come to pass that the Evil One shall fall when he layeth a snare

PLATE 21 81

to destroy me, and may the joints of his neck
and of his back be cut in sunder.

Ra [saileth] with a fair wind, and the
sektet *boat* draweth on and cometh into port.
The mariners of Ra rejoice, and the heart of
Nebt-ankh is glad, for the enemy of her lord
hath fallen to the ground. Thou shalt behold
Horus on the watch [in the Boat], and Thoth
and Maat upon either side of him. All the
gods rejoice when they behold Ra coming
in peace to make the hearts of the shining
ones to live. May Osiris Ani, triumphant, the
scribe of the divine offerings of the lords of
Thebes, be with them.'

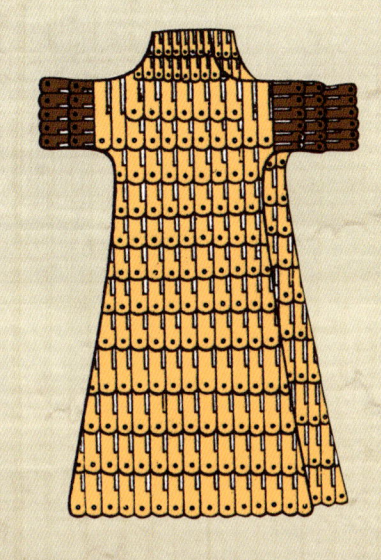

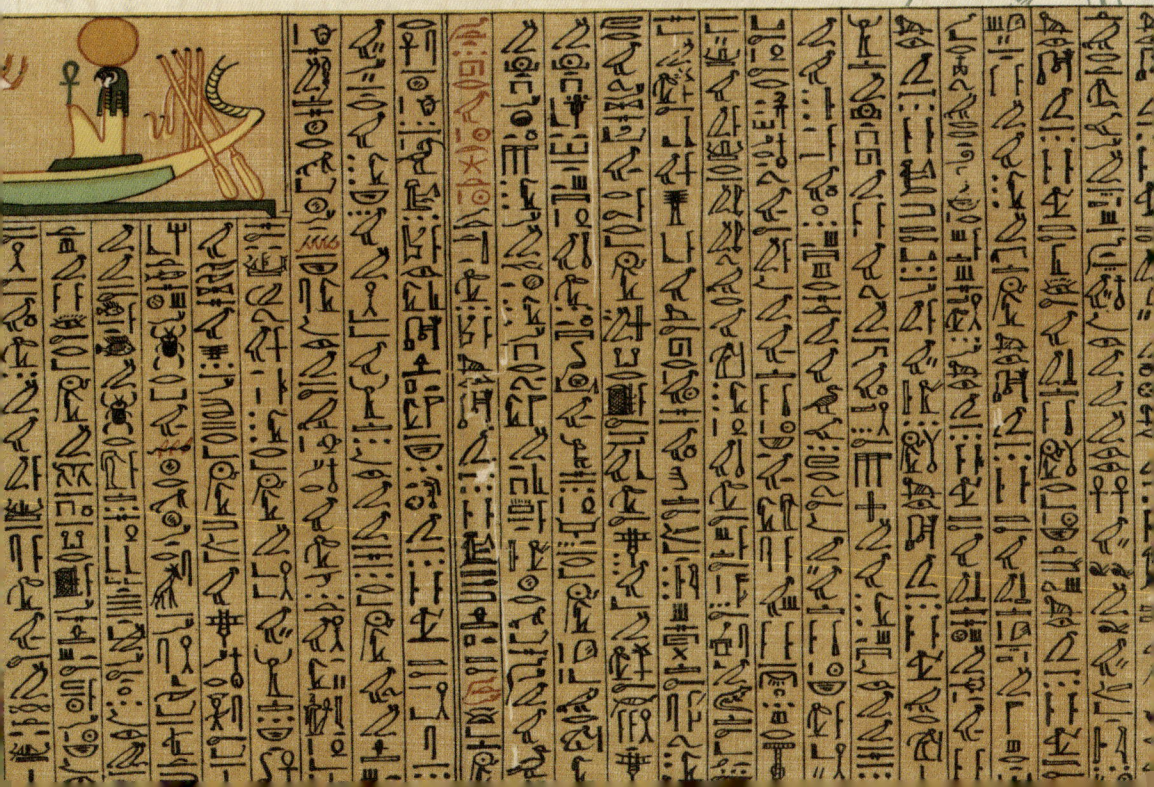

Ra, hawk-headed, with the disk upon his head and the emblem of life upon his knees, seated in the solar bark; before him stands Ani with both hands raised in adoration.

TO BE SAID ON THE DAY OF THE MONTH.[101] *Osiris Ani, the scribe, triumphant in peace, triumphant, saith: 'Ra riseth in his horizon, and the company of his gods follow after the god when he appeareth from his secret place, when he showeth strength and bringeth himself forth from the eastern horizon of heaven at the word of the goddess Nut. They rejoice at the journeyings of Ra, the Ancient One; the Great One rolleth along in his course. Thy joints are knitted together,[102] O Ra, within thy shrine. Thou breathest the winds, thou drawest in the breezes, thou makest thy jaw-bones to eat in thy dwelling on the day when thou dost scent right and truth. Thou turnest aside the godlike followers [who] sail after the sacred boat, in order that they may return again unto the mighty ones according to thy word. Thou numberest thy bones, thou gatherest together thy members; thou turnest thy face towards the beautiful Amenta; thou comest thither renewed day by day. Behold, thou Image of gold, who possessest the splendours of the Disk of heaven, thou lord of terror; thou rollest along and art renewed day by day. Hail, there is rejoicing in the heavenly horizon, and shouts of joy are raised to the ropes which tow thee along. May the gods who dwell in heaven ascribe praises unto Osiris Ani, when they behold him in triumph, as unto Ra. May Osiris, the scribe Ani, be a prince who is known by the ureret crown; and may the meat offerings and the drink offerings of Osiris Ani, triumphant, be apportioned unto him; may he wax exceeding strong in his body; and may he be the chief of those who are in the presence of Ra. May Osiris, the scribe Ani, triumphant, be strong upon earth and in the world under the earth; and O Osiris, scribe Ani, triumphant, mayest thou rise up strengthened like unto Ra day by day. Osiris Ani, triumphant, shall not tarry, nor shall he rest without motion in the earth for ever. Clearly, clearly shall he see with his two eyes, and with his two ears shall be hear what is right and true. Osiris, the scribe Ani, triumphant, cometh back, cometh back from Annu; Osiris Ani, triumphant, is as Ra when he rangeth the oars among the followers of Nu. [Ed: Text continues on next plate].*

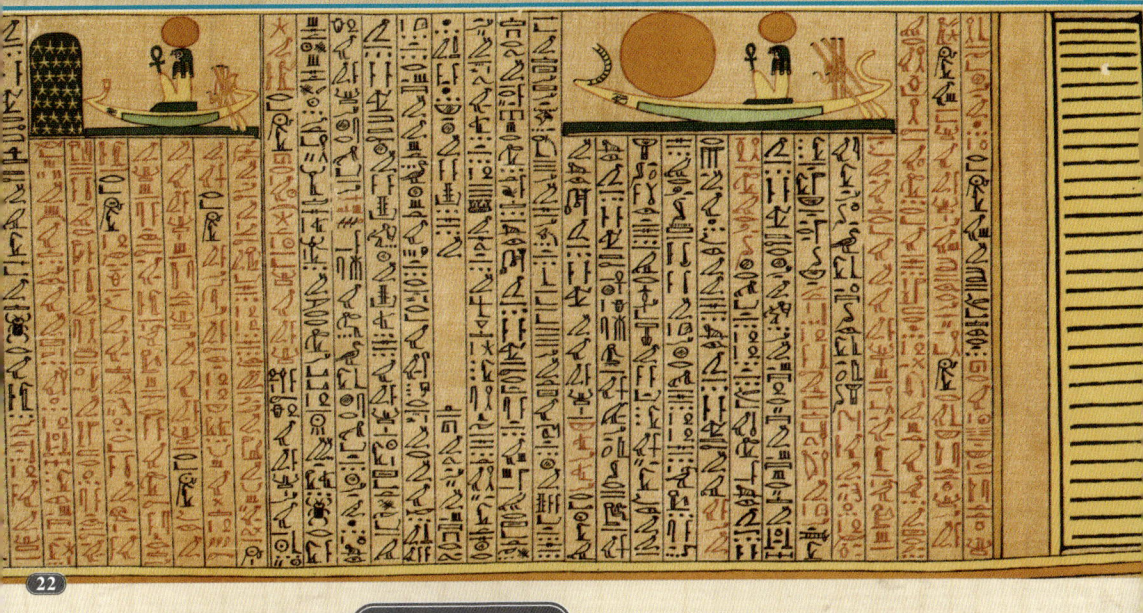

22

PLATE 22

Osiris Ani, triumphant, hath not revealed what he hath seen, he hath not, he hath not told again what he hath heard in the house which is hidden. Hail, there are shouts of joy to Osiris Ani, triumphant, for he is a god and the flesh of Ra, he is in the boat of Nu, and his ka is well pleased according to the will of the god. Osiris Ani, triumphant, is in peace, he is triumphant like unto Horus, and he is mighty because he hath divers forms.'

Ra seated in a boat, sailing across the sky towards the star-studded heaven.

Rubric: These words shall be recited over a boat seven cubits in length, and painted green for the godlike rulers. Then shalt thou make a heaven of stars washed and purified with natron and incense. Behold, thou shalt make an image of Ra upon a table of stone painted yellow (?), and it shall be placed in the fore-part of the boat. Behold, thou shalt make an image of the dead man whom thou wilt make perfect in strength in the boat; and thou shalt make it to travel in the divine

boat of Ra, and Ra himself will look upon it therein. Thou shalt show it to no man but thyself, or to thy father or to thy son; let them watch with their faces, and he shall be seen in the underworld as a messenger of Ra.

Ra, hawk-headed, with a disk upon his head, seated in a boat; before him is a large disk. A HYMN OF PRAISE TO RA ON THE DAY OF THE MONTH WHEREON HE SAILETH IN THE BOAT. *[Osiris, the scribe Ani, saith]: 'Homage to thee, O thou who art in thy boat! Thou risest, thou risest, thou shinest with thy rays, and thou hast made mankind to rejoice for millions of years according to thy will. Thou showest thy face unto the beings whom thou hast created, O Khepera, in thy boat. Thou hast overthrown Apepi. O ye children of Seb, overthrow ye the foes of Osiris Ani, triumphant, destroy ye the adversaries of righteousness from the boat of Ra. Horus shall cut off your heads in heaven in the likeness of ducks; ye shall fall down upon the earth and become beasts, and into the water in the likeness of fishes. [Osiris, the scribe Ani,] destroyeth every hostile fiend, male and female, whether he passeth through heaven, [or] appeareth upon earth, or cometh forth upon the water, or passeth along before the starry deities; and Thoth strengtheneth them… coming forth from Anreti. Osiris, the scribe Ani, is silent, and becometh the second of Ra. Behold thou the god, the great slaughterer, greatly to be feared, he washeth in your blood,*

he batheth in your gore; Osiris, the scribe Ani, destroyeth them from the boat of his father Ra-Horus. The mother Isis giveth birth unto Osiris, the scribe Ani, triumphant, whose heart liveth, and Nephthys nurseth him; even as they did for Horus, who drove back the fiends of Sut. They saw the urertu *crown stablished upon his head, and they fell down upon their faces. Behold, O ye shining ones, ye men and gods, ye damned ones, when ye behold Osiris Ani, triumphant like unto Horus and adored by reason of the* ureret *crown, fall ye down upon your faces; for Osiris Ani is victorious over his foes in the heavens above and [on the earth] beneath, in the presence of the godlike rulers of all the gods and goddesses.'*

Rubric: *These words shall be recited over a great hawk which hath the white crown set upon his head. Then shall the names of Tmu, Shu, Tefnut, Seb, Nut, Osiris, Isis, Nephthys, be written with green colour upon a new table, anointed with unguents and placed in a boat together with a figure of the dead man. Then shall they put incense upon the fire, and set ducks to be roasted. This is a rite of Ra when his boat cometh; and it shall cause the dead man to go with Ra into every place whithersoever he saileth, and the foes of Ra shall be slaughtered in very truth. The chapter of the* sektet *boat shall be recited on the sixth day of the festival.*

The ladder by which the soul passes from the underworld to the body.

PLATES 23 - 24

The whole of Plate 23 and part of Plate 24 (see pages 86–7) contain a repetition of the 18th chapter of the Book of the Dead, which has also been given on Plates 13 and 14. The arrangement of the gods in the vignette is, however, slightly different.

On the right side of Plate 24 are shown Ani and his wife adoring three gods, who are seated on a pylon or door-shaped pedestal.

23

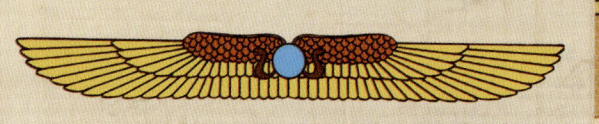

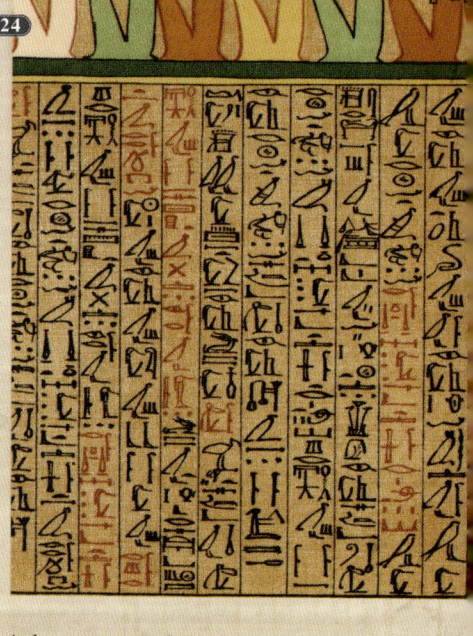

THE CHAPTER OF GOING UNTO THE GODLIKE RULERS OF OSIRIS. *Osiris, the scribe Ani, triumphant, saith: 'My soul hath builded for me a dwelling-place in Tattu. I have waxed strong in the town Pe. I have ploughed [my] fields in all my forms, and my palm tree standeth therein like unto the god Amsu. I eat not that which I abominate, I eat not that which I loathe; that which I abominate I abominate, and I feed not upon filth. There are food offerings and meat for those who shall not be destroyed thereby. I raise not up myself on my two arms unto any abomination, I walk not thereupon with my shoes, because my bread is [made] from white grain, and my ale from the red barley of the Nile. The* sektet *boat and the* atet *boat bring them unto me, and I feed upon them under the trees, whose beautiful branches I myself do know. How glorious do I make the white crown [when] I lift up the uraei! Hail, guardian of the door, who givest peace unto the two lands, bring thou unto me those who make offerings! Grant that I may lift up the earth; that the shining ones may open their arms unto me; that the company of the gods may speak with the words of the shining ones unto Osiris Ani; that the hearts of the gods may direct [him]; and that they may make him powerful in heaven among the gods who have taken unto themselves visible forms. Yea, let every god and every goddess whom he passeth make Osiris, the scribe Ani, triumphant at the new year. He feedeth upon hearts and consumeth them when he cometh forth from the East. He hath been judged by the forefather of light. He is a shining one arrayed in heaven among the mighty ones. The food of Osiris, the scribe Ani, triumphant, is even the cakes and ale which are*

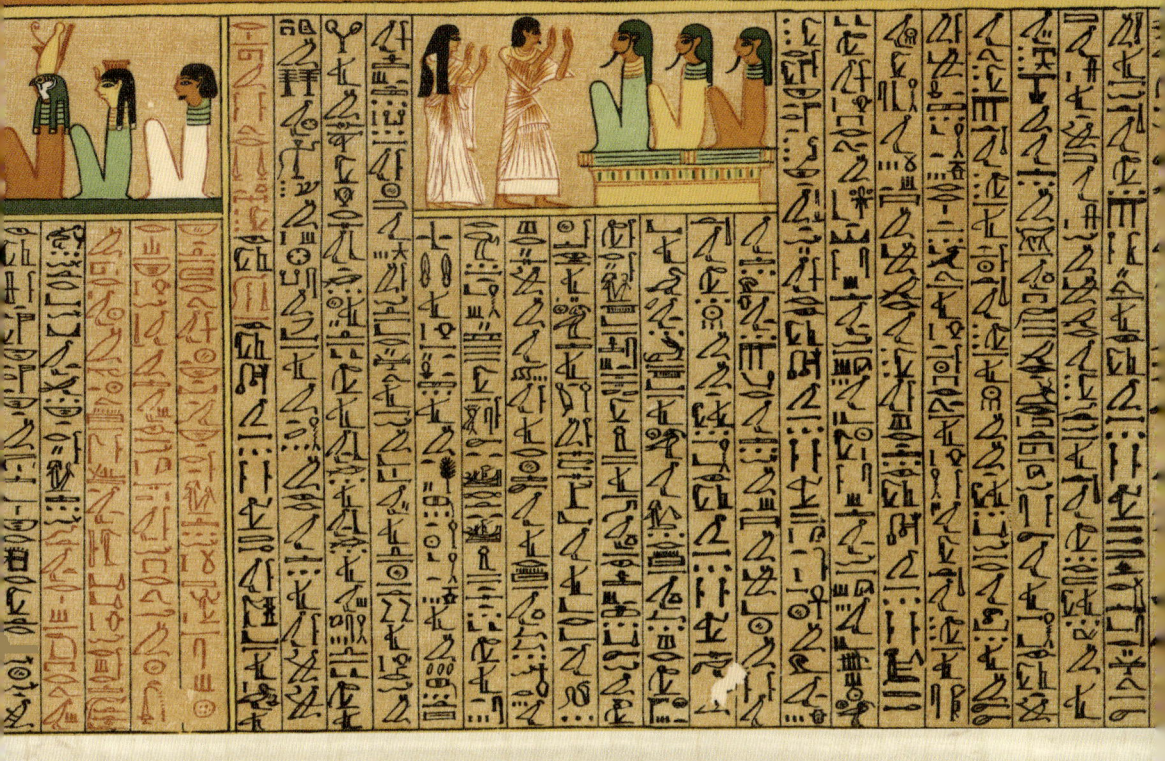

made for their mouths. I go in through the Disk, I come out through the god Ahui. I speak with the followers of the gods, I speak with the Disk, I speak with the shining ones, and the Disk granteth me to be victorious in the blackness of night within Meh-urt near unto his forehead. Behold, I am with Osiris, and I proclaim that which he telleth forth among the mighty ones. He speaketh unto me the words of men, and I listen and I tell again unto him the words of the gods. I, Osiris Ani, triumphant, come even as one who is equipped for the journey. Thou raisest up [right and truth] for those who love them. I am a shining one clothed in power, mightier than any other shining one.'

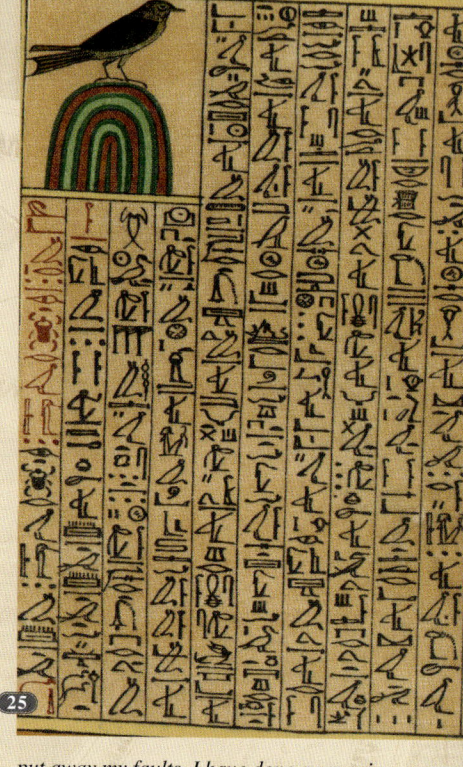

PLATE 25

A swallow perched on a conical object painted red and green.

HERE BEGIN THE CHAPTERS OF MAKING TRANSFORMATIONS. THE CHANGING INTO A SWALLOW. *Saith Osiris Ani, triumphant: 'I am the swallow, [I am] the swallow, [I am] the scorpion, the daughter of Ra. Hail, ye gods, whose scent is sweet; hail, ye gods, whose scent is sweet! Hail, thou Flame, which comest forth from the horizon! Hail, thou who art in the city. May the Guardian of the Bight lead me on. O stretch out up unto me thine bands that I may be able to pass my days in the Island of Flame. I have fared forth with my warrant. I have come with the power thereof. Let the doors be opened unto me. How shall I tell what I have seen therein? Horus was like unto the prince of the sacred bark, and the throne of his father was given unto him. Sut, the son of Nut, also hath gotten the fall which he wrought for Horus. He who is in Sekhem passed judgment upon me. I stretched out my hands and my arms unto Osiris. I have passed on to judgment, and I have come that I may speak; grant that I may pass on and deliver my message. I enter in, having been judged; I come out at the door of Neb-er-tcher magnified and glorified. I am found pure at the great place of passage [of souls]. I have*  *put away my faults. I have done away mine offences. I have cast out the sins which were a part of me. I, even I, am pure, I, even I, am mighty. O ye doorkeepers, I have made my way [unto you]. I am like unto you. I have come forth by day. I have walked with my legs, and I have gotten the power of the footstep wherewith do walk the shining ones of light. I, even I, know the hidden ways to the doors of the Field of Aaru; and, though my body be buried, yet let me rise up; and may I come forth and overthrow all my foes upon earth.'*

PLATE 25

89

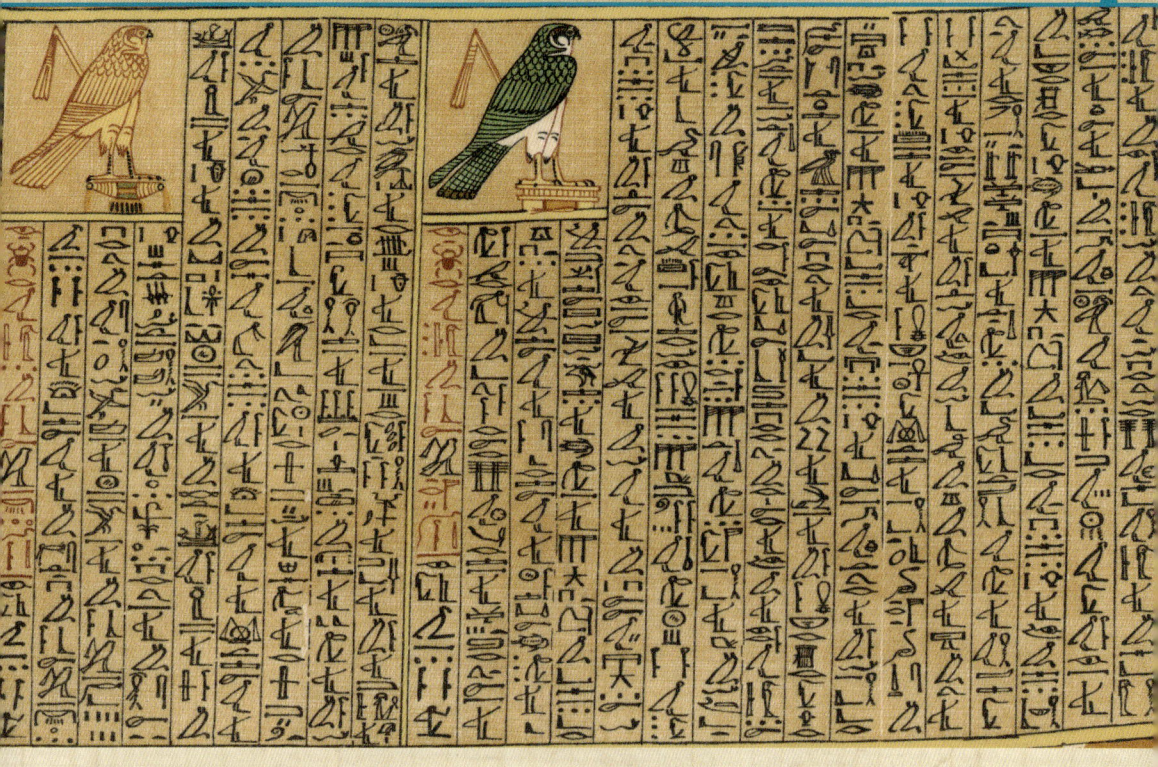

Rubric: If this chapter be known [by the deceased], he shall come forth by day in Neter-khert, and he shall go in again after he hath come forth. If this chapter be not known, he shall not enter in after he hath come forth, nor shall he come forth by day.

A golden hawk holding a flail, emblem of rule.

CHAPTER OF CHANGING INTO A GOLDEN HAWK. *Saith Osiris Ani: 'May I, even I, arise in the* seshet *chamber, like unto a hawk*

of gold coming forth from his egg. May I fly and may I hover as a hawk, with a back seven cubits wide, and with wings made of emeralds of the South. May I come forth from the sektet *boat, and may my heart be brought unto me from the mountain of the East. May I alight on the* atet *boat, and may those who are in their companies be brought unto me, bowing down as they come. May I rise, may I gather myself together as the beautiful golden hawk [which hath] the head of a* bennu *bird. May I enter into the presence of Ra daily to*

hear his words, and may I sit down among the mighty gods of Nut. May a homestead be made ready for me, and may offerings of food and drink be put before me therein. May I eat therein; may I become a shining one therein; may I be filled therein to my heart's fullest desire; may sacred wheat be given unto me to eat. May I, by myself, get power over the guardian of my head.'

A green hawk, holding a flail, and standing upon a pylon-shaped pedestal.

THE CHAPTER OF BECOMING INTO A SACRED HAWK. *Saith Osiris Ani: 'Hail, thou mighty one, come unto Tattu. Make thou my paths, and let me pass round [to visit] my thrones. Make me to renew myself and make me to wax strong. Grant that I may be feared, and make me to be a terror. May the gods of the underworld fear me, and may they fight for me in their habitations. Let not him that would do harm unto me draw nigh unto me. Let me walk through the house of darkness. May I, the feeble, clothe and cover myself; and may they (i.e. the gods) not do the like unto me. Hail, ye gods who hear my speech! Hail, ye rulers who are among the followers of Osiris. Be ye therefore silent, O ye gods, [when] the god speaketh with me; he heareth what is right and true. What I speak unto him, do thou also speak, O Osiris. Grant thou that I may go round my course according to the order which cometh forth from thy mouth concerning me. May I see thy forms; may I be able to understand thy will. Grant that I may come forth, that I may get power over my legs, and that I may be like unto Neb-er-tcher upon his throne. May the gods of the underworld fear me, and may they fight for me in their habitations. Grant thou that I may pass on my way with the godlike ones who rise up. May I be set up upon my resting place like unto the Lord of Life; may I be joined unto Isis, the divine Lady. May the gods make me strong against him that would do harm unto me, and may no one come to see me fall helpless. May I pass over the paths, may I come into the furthermost parts of heaven. I entreat for speech with Seb, I make supplication unto Hu and unto Neb-er-tcher that the gods of the underworld may fear me, and that they may fight for me in their habitations, when they see that thou hast provided me with the fowl of the air and the fish of the sea.*

I am one of those shining ones who live in rays of light. I have made my form like unto the form [of the god] who cometh out and manifesteth himself in Tattu; for I have become worthy of honour by reason of his honour, and he hath spoken unto thee of the things which concern me. Surely he hath made the fear of me

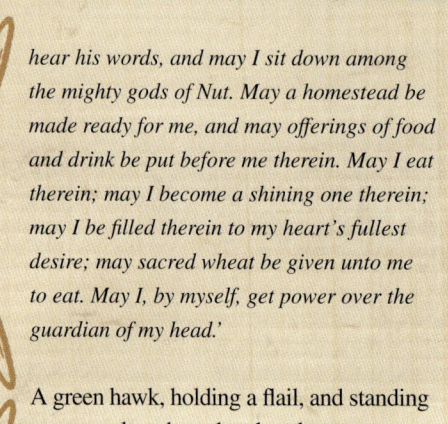

PLATE 26

[to go forth], and hath created terror of me! The gods of the… [Ed: Text continues on next plate]

'… underworld fear me, and they fight for me [in their habitations]. I, in very truth, I am a shining one and a dweller in light, who hath been created and who hath come into being from the body of the god. I am one of the shining ones who dwell in light, whom Tmu himself hath created, and who have come into being from the eyelashes of his eye. He doth create and glorify and make noble the faces of those who live with him. Behold, the only One in Nu! They do homage unto him as he cometh forth from the horizon, and they strike fear of him into the gods and into the shining ones who have come into being with him.

I am the One among the worms which the eye of the Lord, the only One, hath created. And lo! before Isis was, and when Horus was not yet, I had waxed strong and flourished. I had grown old, and I had become greater than

they who were among the shining ones who had come into being with him, and I, even I, arose in the form of a sacred hawk, and Horus made me worthy in the form of his own soul, to take possession of all that belongeth unto Osiris in the underworld. The double Lion-god, the warder of the things that belong to the house of the nemmes crown which is in his hiding place, saith unto me: "Get thee back to the heights of heaven, seeing that through Horus thou hast become glorified in thy form; the nemmes crown is not for thee; thou hast speech even unto the ends of heaven." I, the guardian, take possession of the things which belong to Horus and Osiris in the underworld. Horus telleth aloud unto me that which his father had said concerning me in years [gone by], on the day of the burial [of Osiris]. I have given unto thee the nemmes of the double Lion-god which I possess, that thou mayest pass onward and mayest travel over the path of heaven, and that they who dwell on the

confines of the horizon may see thee, and that the gods of the underworld may fear thee and may fight for thee in their habitations. The god Auhet is of them. The gods, the lords of the boundaries of heaven, they who are the warders of the shrine of the lord, the only One, have fallen before my words, have fallen down before [my] words. Hail! He that is exalted upon his tomb is on my side, and he hath bound upon my head the nemmes crown. The double Lion-god hath decreed it, the god Auhet hath made a way for me. I, even I, am exalted, and the double Lion-god hath bound the nemmes crown on me, and my head covering hath been given unto me. He hath stablished my heart through his strength and through his great might, and I shall not fall through Shu. I am Hetep, the lord of the two uraei, the being who is adored. I know the shining god, and his breath is in my body. I shall not be driven back

by the Bull which causeth men to tremble, but I shall come daily into the house of the double Lion-god, and I shall come forth therefrom into the house of Isis. I shall behold sacred things which are hidden, there shall be done unto me holy hidden rites. I shall see what is there; my words shall make full the majesty of Shu, and they shall drive away evil hap. I, even I, am Horus who dwell in splendours. I have gained power over his crown, I have gained power over his radiance, and I have travelled over the remotest parts of heaven. Horus is upon his throne, Horus is upon his seat. My face is like unto that of a divine hawk. I am one who hath been armed by his lord. I have come forth from Tattu. I have seen Osiris, I have risen up on either side of him. Nut [hath shrouded me]. The gods behold me, and I have beheld the gods. The eye of Horus hath consumed me, who dwell in darkness. The gods stretch forth

PLATE 26   93

their arms unto me. I rise up, I get the mastery, and I drive back evil which opposeth me. The gods open unto me the holy way, they see my form, and they hear my words which I utter in their presence. O ye gods of the underworld, who set yourselves up against me, and who resist the mighty ones, the stars which never set have led me on my way. I have passed along the holy paths of the hemtet *chamber unto your lord, the exceedingly mighty and terrible Soul. Horus hath commanded that ye lift up your faces to look upon me. I have risen up in the likeness of a divine hawk, and Horus hath set me apart in the likeness of his own soul, to take possession of that which belongeth unto Osiris in the underworld. I have passed along the way, I have travelled on and I have come even among those who live in their hiding places and who guard the house of Osiris. I speak unto them of his power and I make*

them to know the terrible power of him that is provided with two horns [to fight] against Sut; and they know who hath carried off the sacred food which the power (?) of Tmu had brought for him. The gods of the underworld have proclaimed a happy coming for me. O Ye who live in your hiding places and who guard the house of Osiris, and who have magnified your names, grant ye that I may come unto you. I bind together and I gather up your powers, and I order the strength of the paths of those who guard the horizon of the hemtet *of heaven. I have stablished their habitations for Osiris, I have ordered his ways, I have done what hath been bidden. I have come forth from Tattu, I have beheld Osiris, I have spoken unto him concerning the things of his son, the divine Prince whom he loveth. There is a wound in the heart of Set, and I have seen him who is without…[Ed: text continues on next plate]*

PLATE 27

... *life. O, I have made them to know the plans of the gods which Horus hath devised at the bidding of his father Osiris. Hail, lord, thou most terrible and mighty soul! Let me come, even me, let me lift myself up! I have opened and passed through the underworld. I have opened the paths of the warders of heaven and of the warders of the earth. I have not been driven back by them; and I have lifted up thy face, O lord of eternity.'*

The serpent Seta, with human legs.

THE CHAPTER OF CHANGING INTO SETA. *Osiris Ani, triumphant, saith: 'I am the serpent Seta, whose years are many. I lie down and I am born day by day. I am the serpent Seta, which dwelleth in the limits of the earth. I lie down, I am born, I renew myself, I grow young day by day.'*

A crocodile upon a pylon or doorway.

THE CHAPTER OF CHANGING INTO A CROCODILE. *Saith Osiris Ani, triumphant: 'I am the crocodile which dwelleth in terror, I am the sacred crocodile and I cause destruction. I am the great fish in Kamui. I am the lord to whom homage is paid in Sekhem; and Osiris Ani is the lord to whom homage is paid in Sekhem.'*

The god Ptah in a shrine, before which is a table of offerings.

THE CHAPTER OF CHANGING INTO PTAH. *Saith Osiris Ani, triumphant: 'I eat bread, I drink ale, I put on apparel, I fly like a hawk, I cackle like a goose, and I alight upon the path hard by the hill of the dead on the festival of the great Being. That which is abominable, that which is abominable, have I not eaten; and that which is foul have I not swallowed. That which my ka doth abominate hath not entered into my body. I have lived according to the knowledge of the glorious gods. I live and I get strength from their bread, I get strength when I eat it beneath the shade of the tree of Hathor, my lady. I make an offering, and I make bread in Tattu, and*

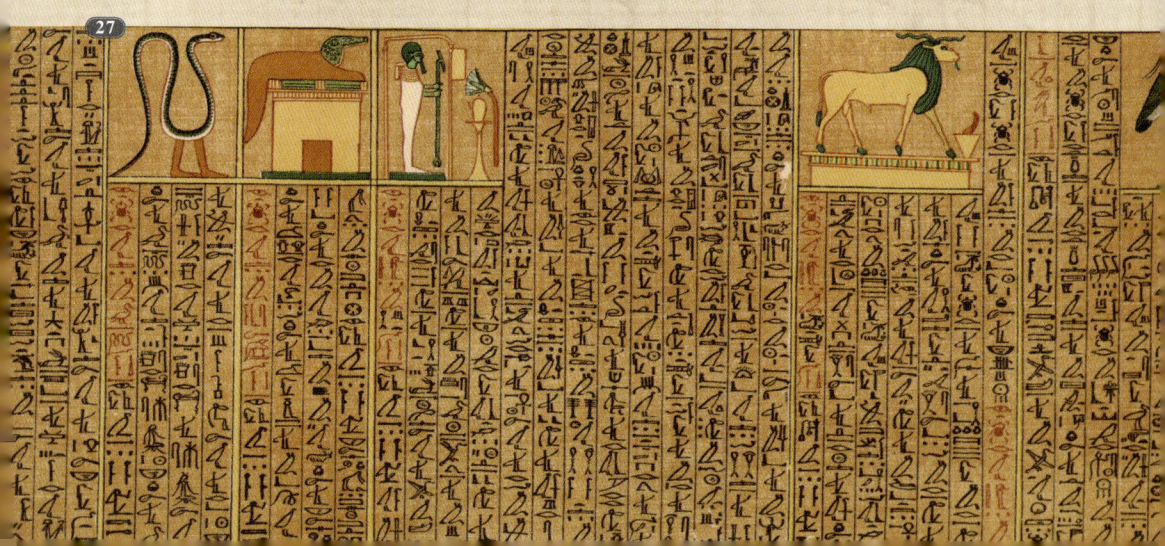

27

PLATE 27 95

oblations in Annu. I array myself in the robe of the goddess Matait, and I rise up and I sit me down wheresoever my heart desireth. My head is like unto the head of Ra; when my limbs are gathered together, I am like unto Tmu. The four regions of Ra are the limits of the earth. I come forth; my tongue is like unto the tongue of Ptah, my throat is even as that of Hathor, and I tell forth the words of my father Tmu with my lips. He it is who constrained the handmaid, the wife of Seb; and unto him are bowed [all] heads, and there is fear of him. Hymns of praise are sung in honour of my mighty deeds, and I am accounted the heir of Seb, the lord of the earth, the protector. The god Seb giveth cool water, he maketh his dawnings to be mine. They who dwell in Annu bow down their heads before me, for I am their Bull. I grow strong from moment to moment; my loins are made strong for millions of years.'

A Ram.

THE CHAPTER OF CHANGING INTO THE SOUL OF TMU. *Saith Osiris Ani, triumphant:* 'I have not entered into the house of destruction; I have not been brought to naught, I have not known decay. I am Ra who come forth from Nu, the divine Soul, the creator of his own limbs. Sin is an abomination unto me, and I look not thereon; I cry not out against right and truth, but I have my being therein. I am the god Hu, and I never die in my name of "Soul". I have brought myself into being together with Nu in my name

of "Khepera". In their forms have I come into being in the likeness of Ra. I am the lord of light.'

A *bennu* bird.

THE CHAPTER OF CHANGING INTO A BENNU. *Saith Osiris, the scribe Ani, triumphant in peace:* 'I came into being from unformed matter, I created myself in the image of the god Khepera, and I grew in the form of plants. I am hidden in the likeness of the Tortoise. I am formed out of the atoms of all the gods. I am the yesterday of the four [quarters of the world], and I am the seven uraei which came into existence in the East, the mighty one who illumineth the nations by his body. He is god in the likeness of Set; and Thoth dwelleth in the midst of them by judgment of the dweller in Sekhem and of the spirits of Annu. I sail among them, and I come; I am crowned, I am become a shining one, I am mighty, I am become holy among the gods. I am the god Khonsu who driveth back all that opposeth him.'

[Appendix[103]] **Rubric**: If this chapter be known, the purified one shall come forth by day after his burial, and he shall change his forms at his heart's desire. He shall dwell among the servants of Un-nefer, and he shall be satisfied with the food of Osiris, and with the meals of the tomb. He shall behold the Disk of the Sun, and shall travel over the earth with Ra. He shall be triumphant before Osiris, and there shall no evil thing get dominion over him for ever and for all eternity and for ever.

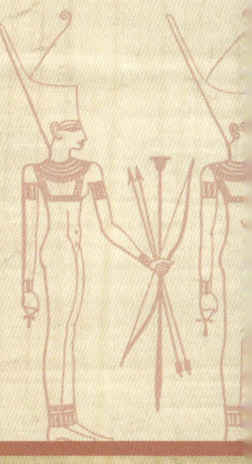

PLATE 28

A heron.

THE CHAPTER OF CHANGING INTO A HERON. *Saith Osiris, the scribe Ani: 'I have gotten dominion over the beasts which are brought for sacrifice, with the knife held at their heads and their hair, for those who dwell in their emerald [fields], the ancient and the shining ones who make ready the hour of Osiris Ani, triumphant in peace. He maketh slaughter upon earth, and I make slaughter upon earth. I am strong, and I have passed along the lofty path [which leadeth] unto heaven. I have made myself pure, with long strides I have gone unto my city, holding on my way to Sepu (?). I have stablished [the one who is] in Unnu. I have set the gods upon their places, and I have made glorious the temples of those who live in their shrines. I know the goddess Nut, I know the god Tatunen, I know Teshert, I have brought with me their horns. I know Heka, I have heard his words, I am the red calf which is limned with the pen. When they hear [my words], the gods say: "Let us bow down our faces, and let him come unto us; the light shineth beyond you." My hour is within my body. I have not spoken [evil] in the place of right and truth, and each day I advance in right and truth. I am shrouded in darkness when I sail up to celebrate the festival of the dead one, and to embalm the Aged one, the guardian of the earth – I the Osiris, the scribe Ani, triumphant! I have not entered into the hiding places of the starry deities. I have ascribed glory unto Osiris. I have pacified the heart of the gods who follow after him. I have not felt fear of those who cause terror, even those who dwell in their own lands. Behold, I am exalted upon [my] resting place upon my throne. I am Nu, and I shall never be overthrown by the Evil-doer. I am the god Shu who sprang from unformed matter. My soul is god; my soul is eternity. I am the creator of darkness, and I appoint unto it a resting place in the uttermost parts of heaven. I am the prince of eternity, I am the exalted one [in] Nebu. I grow young in [my] city, I grow young in my homestead. My name is "Never-failing". My name is "Soul, Creator of Nu, who maketh his abode in the underworld." My nest is not seen, and I have not broken my egg. I am Lord of Millions of Years- I have made my nest in the uttermost parts of heaven. I have come down unto the earth of Seb. I have done away with my faults. I have seen my father as the lord of Shautat. As concerning Osiris Ani, may his body dwell in Annu; may it be manifested unto those who are with the shining one in the place of burial in Amenta…'*

A human head springing from a lotus in a pool of water.

[THE CHAPTER OF] CHANGING INTO A LOTUS. *Saith Osiris Ani: 'I am the pure lotus which cometh forth from the god of light, the guardian of the nostrils of Ra, the guardian of the nose of Hathor. I advance*

PLATE 28 97

and I hasten after him who is Horus. I am, the pure one who cometh forth from the field.'

A god with a disk upon his head.

[THE CHAPTER OF] CHANGING INTO THE GOD WHO GIVETH LIGHT IN THE DARKNESS. *Saith Osiris, the scribe Ani, triumphant: 'I am the girdle of the robe of the god Nu, which shineth and sheddeth light, which abideth in his presence and sendeth forth light into the darkness, which knitteth together the two fighters who live in my body through the mighty spell of the words of my mouth, which raiseth up him that hath fallen – for he who was with him in the valley of Abtu hath fallen – and I rest. I have remembered him. I have carried away the god Hu from my city wherein I found him, and I have led away the darkness captive by my might. I have upheld the Eye [of the Sun] when its power waned at the coming of the festival of the fifteenth day, and I have weighed Sut in the heavenly mansions beside the Aged one who is with him. I have endowed Thoth in the House of the Moon-god with all that is needful for the coming of the festival of the fifteenth day. I have carried off the* ureret *crown; right and truth are in my body. The months are of emerald and crystal. My homestead is among the sapphire furrows. I am the lady who sheddeth light in darkness. I have come to give forth light in darkness, and lo! it is lightened and made bright. I have illumined the blackness and I have overthrown the destroyers. I have made obeisance unto those who are in darkness, and I have raised up those who wept and who had hidden their faces and had sunk down. Then did they look upon me. I am the Lady, and I will not let you hear concerning me.'*

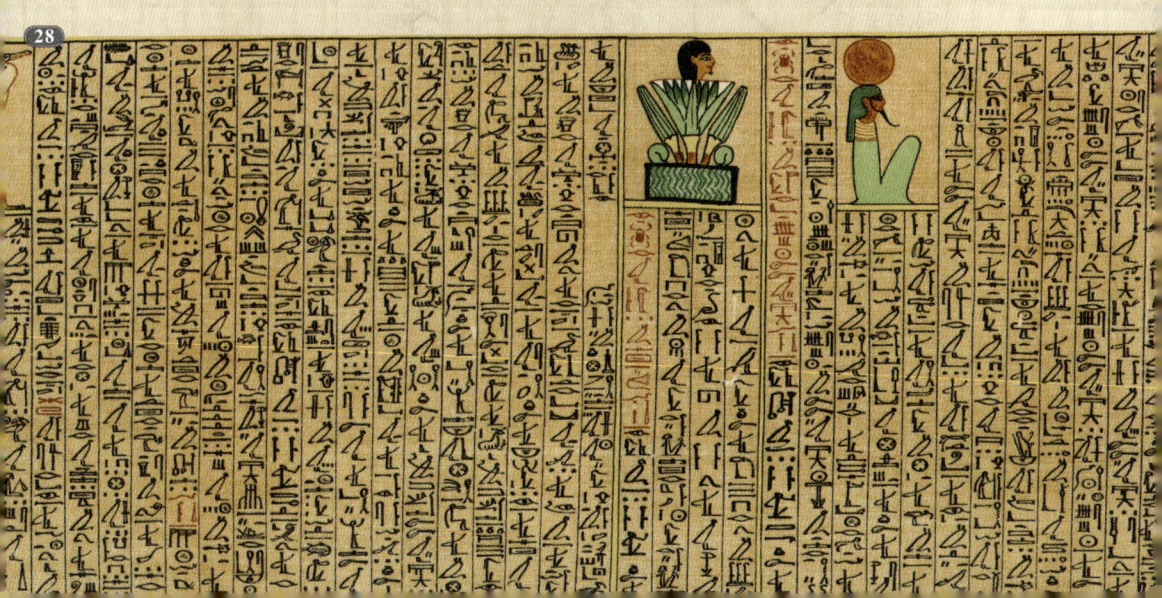

PLATES 29-30

Ani and his wife standing with hands raised in adoration before the god Thoth, who has *ankh*, 'life', upon his knees, and is seated on a pylon-shaped throne.

THE CHAPTER OF NOT DYING A SECOND TIME. *Saith Osiris Ani, triumphant: 'Hail, Thoth! What is it that hath happened unto the holy children of Nut? They have done battle, they have upheld strife, they have done evil, they have created the fiends, they have made slaughter, they have caused trouble; in truth, in all their doings the mighty have worked against the weak. Grant, O might of Thoth, that that which the god Tmu hath decreed [may be done]! And thou regardest not evil, nor art thou provoked to anger when they bring their years to confusion and throng in and push to disturb their months; for in all that they have done unto thee they have worked iniquity in secret. I am thy writing palette, O Thoth, and I have brought unto thee thine ink jar. I am not of those who work iniquity in their secret places; let not evil happen unto me.'*

Saith Osiris, the scribe Ani: 'Hail, Tmu! What manner [of land] is this into which I have come? It hath not water, it hath not air; it is deep unfathomable, it is black as the blackest night, and men wander helplessly therein. In it a man may not live in quietness of heart; nor may the longings of love be satisfied therein. But let the state of the shining ones be given unto me for water and for air and for the satisfying of the longings of love, and let quietness of heart be given unto me for bread and for ale. The god Tmu hath decreed that I shall see his face, and that I shall not suffer from the things which pain him. May the gods hand on their thrones for millions of years. Thy throne hath descended unto thy son Horus. The god Tmu hath decreed that his course shall be among the holy princes. In truth, he shall rule over thy throne, and he shall be heir of the throne of the dweller in the Lake of Fire. It hath been decreed that in me he shall see his likeness, and that my face shall look upon the lord Tmu. How long then have I to live? It is decreed that thou shalt live for millions of millions of years, a life of millions of years. May it be granted that I pass on unto the holy princes, for I am doing away with all that I did when this earth came into being from Nu, and when it sprang from the watery

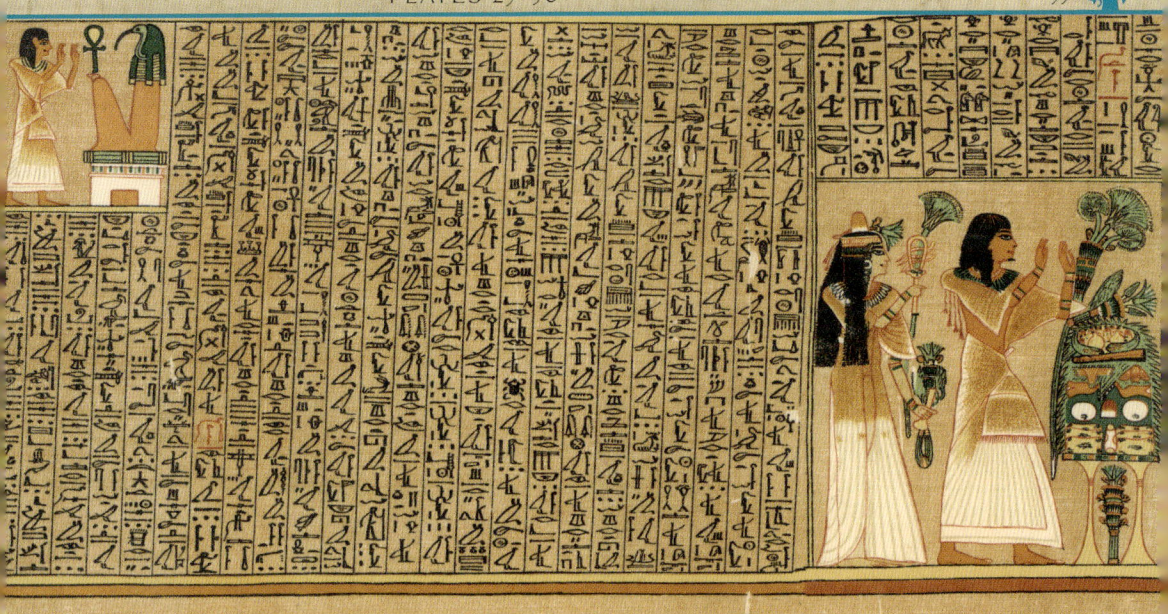

29

abyss even as it was in the days of old. I am
Fate (?) and Osiris, and I have changed my
form into the likeness of divers serpents.
Man knoweth not, and the gods cannot see,
the two-fold beauty which I have made for
Osiris, who is greater than all the gods. I
have granted that he [shall rule] in the mount
of the dead. Verily his son Horus is seated
upon the throne of the dweller in the double
Lake of Fire, as his heir. I have set his throne
in the boat of millions of years. Horus is
established upon his throne, amid the friends
[of Osiris] and all that belonged unto him.
Verily the soul of Sut, which is greater than

all the gods, hath departed to [Amenta]. May
it be granted that I bind his soul in the divine
boat at my will... O my Osiris, thou hast done
for me that which thy father Ra did for thee.
May I abide upon the earth lastingly; may I
keep possession of my throne; may my heir
be strong; may my tomb and my friends who
are upon earth flourish; may my enemies be
given over to destruction and to the shackles
of the goddess Serq! I am thy son, and Ra is
my father. For me likewise hast thou made
life, strength and health. Horus is established
upon his throne. Grant that the days of my life
may come unto worship and honour.'

Ani and his wife Thuthu standing, with hands raised in adoration to Osiris, before a table of offerings.

THE CHAPTER OF ENTERING INTO THE HALL OF DOUBLE RIGHT AND TRUTH: A HYMN OF PRAISE TO OSIRIS, THE DWELLER IN AMENTET. *Osiris, the scribe Ani, triumphant, saith: 'I have come and I have drawn nigh to see thy beauties; my two hands are raised in adoration of thy name Right and Truth. I have drawn nigh unto the place where the acacia tree groweth not, where the tree thick with leaves existeth not, and where the ground yieldeth neither herb nor grass. And I have entered in unto the place of secret and hidden things, I have held converse with the god Sut... Osiris, the scribe Ani, hath entered into the House of Osiris, and he hath seen the hidden and secret things which are therein. The holy rulers of the pylons are in the form of shining ones. Anubis spake unto him with the speech of man when he came from Ta-mera, saying, "He knoweth our paths and our cities, I have been pacified, and the smell of him is to me even as the smell of one of you."'*

Ani saith unto him: 'I am Osiris, the scribe Ani, triumphant in peace, triumphant! I have drawn nigh to behold the great gods, and I feed upon the meals of sacrifice whereon their kas feed. I have been to the boundaries [of the lands] of the Ram, the lord of Tattu, and he hath granted that I may come forth as a bennu *bird and that I may have the power of speech. I have passed through the river-flood. I have made offerings with incense. I have made my way by the side of the thick-leaved tree of the children (?). I have been in Abtu in the House of Satet. I have flooded and I have sunk the boat of my enemies. I have sailed forth upon the Lake in the* neshem *boat. I have seen the noble ones of Kam-ur. I have been in Tattu, and I have constrained myself to silence. I have set the divine Form upon his two feet. I have been with the god Pa-tep-tu-f, and I have seen the dweller in the Holy Temple. I have entered into the House of Osiris, and I have arrayed myself in the apparel of him who is therein. I have entered into Re-stau, and I have beheld the hidden things which are therein. I have been swathed, but I found for myself a thoroughfare. I have entered into An-aarut-f, and I have clothed my body with the apparel which is therein. The* antu *unguent of women hath been given unto me... Verily, Sut spake unto me the things which concern himself, and I said, "Let the thought of the trial of the balance by thee be even within our hearts."'*

The majesty of the god Anubis saith: 'Dost thou know the name of this door to declare it unto me?' Osiris, the scribe Ani, triumphant, triumphant in peace, saith: '"Driven away of Shu" is the name of this door.' Saith the majesty of the god Anubis: 'Dost thou know the name of the upper leaf and of the lower leaf thereof?'

[Osiris, the scribe Ani, triumphant in peace saith]: '"Lord of right and truth, [standing] upon his two feet" is the name of the upper leaf, and "Lord of might and power, dispenser of cattle" [is the name of the lower leaf].' [The majesty of the god Anubis saith]: 'Pass thou, for thou knowest [the names], O Osiris, the scribe, teller of the divine offerings of all the gods of Thebes, Ani, triumphant, lord to be revered.'

The god Osiris, bearded and wearing the white crown, stands in a shrine, the roof of which is surmounted by a hawk's head and uraei; at the back of his neck hangs the *menat*, and in his hands he holds the crook, sceptre, and flail, emblems of royalty, power, and dominion. Behind him stands the goddess Isis, who rests her right hand upon his right shoulder; in her left hand she holds the sign of life. Before Osiris, upon a lotus flower, stand the four children of Horus, the gods of the cardinal points, Mestha, Hapi, Tuamautef, and Qebhsennuf.

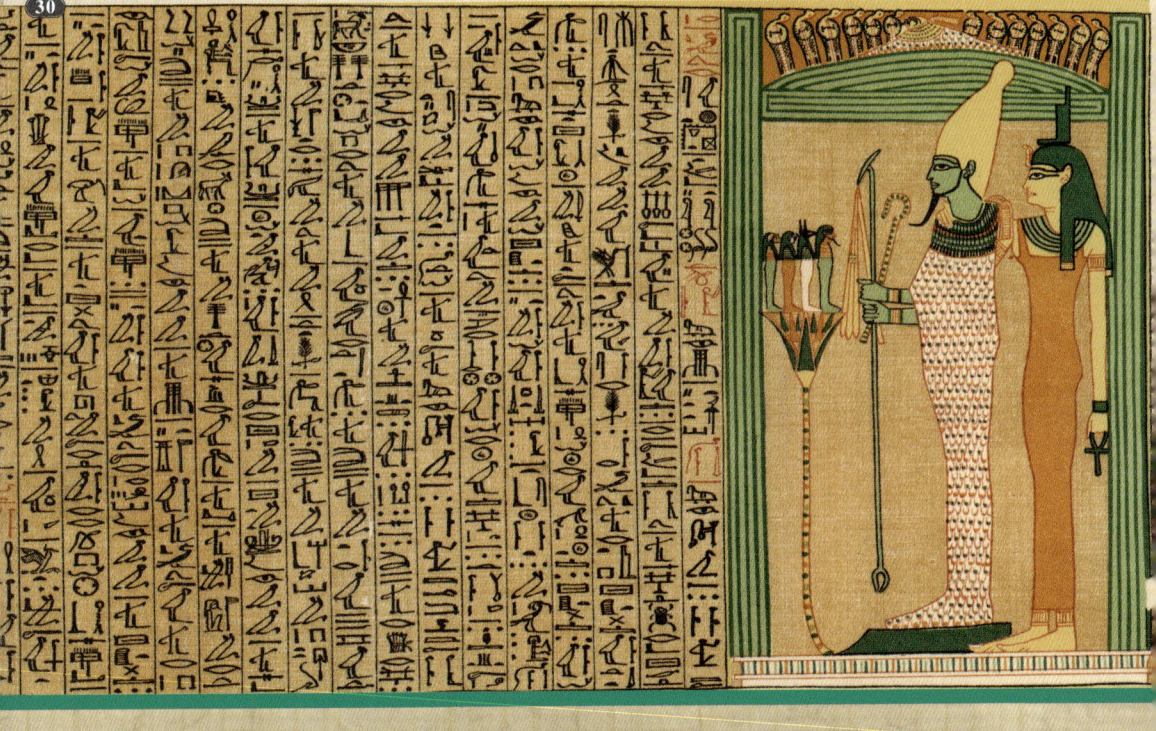

PLATES 31-32

A cross these plates is shown the Hall of Double Right and Truth, wherein Ani has to address severally the forty-two gods, who are seated in a row in the middle of the hall. At each end is a door: that on the right is called 'Neb-Maat-heri-tep-retui-f' and that on the left 'Neb-pehti-thesu-menment'. On the centre of the roof, which is crowned with a series of uraei and feathers emblematic of Maat, is a seated deity with hands extended, the right over the eye of Horus and the left over a pool. On the right, at the end of the hall (Plate 32), are four small vignettes in which are depicted: (1) Two seated figures of the goddess Maat, with [a feather] emblematic of Right and Truth, on the head, and sceptres and emblems of life in the right and left hands. (2) Osiris, seated, wearing the *atef* crown, and holding in his hands the crook and flail. Before him, by the side of an altar of offerings, stands Ani, with both hands raised in adoration. (3) A balance with the heart, symbolizing the conscience of Ani, in one scale, and [a feather] emblematic of Right and Truth, in the other. Beside the balance is the tri-formed monster Amemit. (4) Thoth, ibis-headed, seated on a pylon-shaped pedestal, painting a large feather of Maat.

31

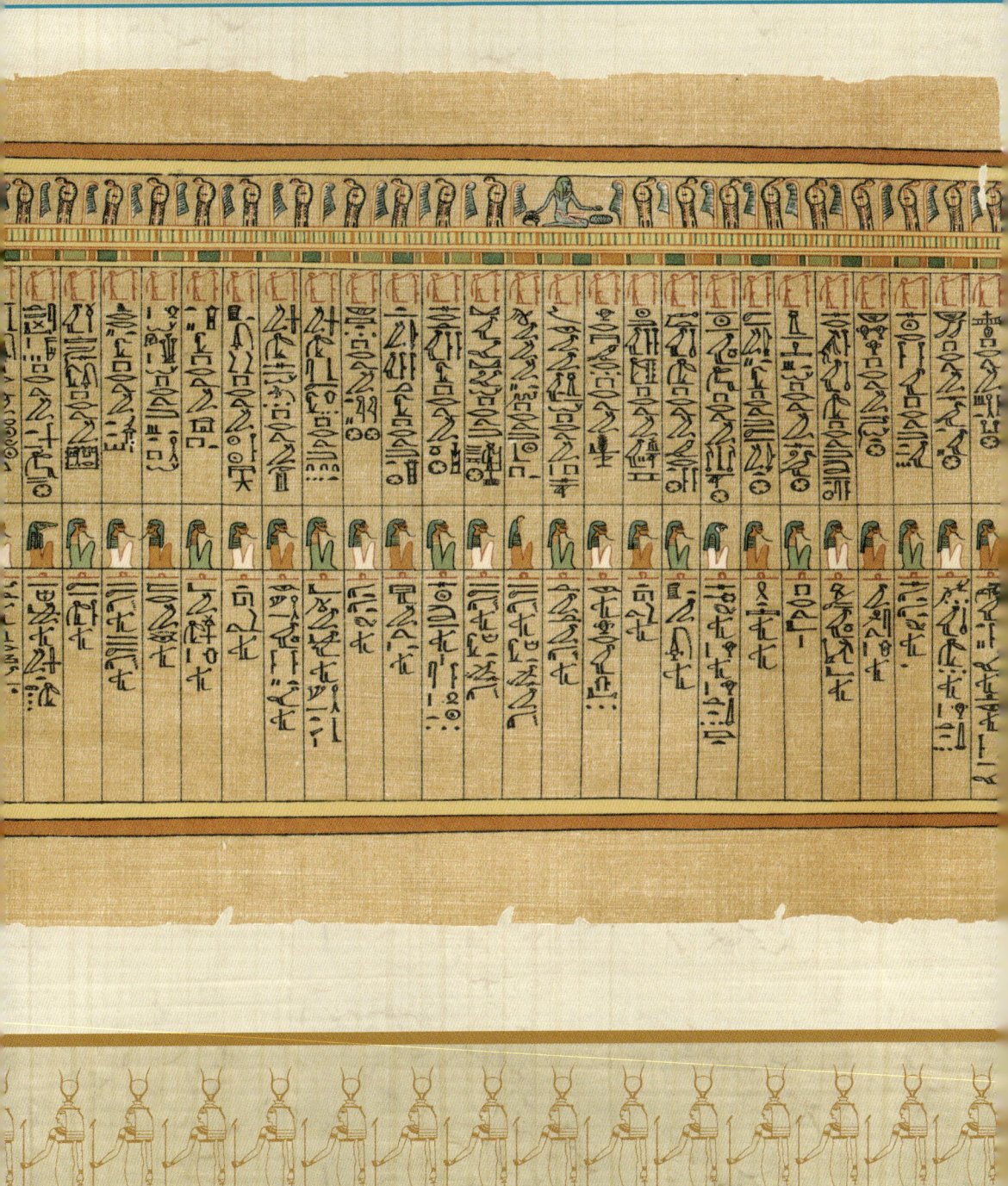

The god Nu.
The hair of Osiris Ani, triumphant, is the hair of Nu.

Ra, hawk-headed, and wearing a disk.
The face of Osiris, the scribe Ani, is the face of Ra.

The goddess Hathor, wearing disk and horns.
The eyes of Osiris Ani, triumphant, are the eyes of Hathor.

The god Ap-uat and standard.
The ears of Osiris Ani, triumphant, are the ears of Ap-uat.

The god Anpu, jackal-headed.
The lips of Osiris Ani, triumphant, are the lips of Anpu.

The scorpion Serqet, holding the *shen*, **and** *ankh*.
The teeth of Osiris Ani, triumphant, are the teeth of Serqet.

The goddess Isis.
The neck of Osiris Ani, triumphant, is the neck of Isis.

The ram-headed god, with uraeus between the horns.
The hands of Osiris Ani, triumphant, are the hands of the Ram, the lord of Tattu.

The god Uatchit, serpent-headed.
The shoulder of Osiris Ani, triumphant, is the shoulder of Uatchit.

The goddess Mert, with outstretched hands, standing upon the emblem of gold, and having on her head a cluster of plants.
The throat of Osiris Ani, triumphant, is the blood of Mert.

The goddess Neith.
The forearms of Osiris Ani, triumphant, are the forearms of the lady of Sais.

The god Sut.
The backbone of Osiris Ani, triumphant, is the backbone of Sut.

A god.
The chest of Osiris Ani, triumphant, is the chest of the lords of Kher-aba.

A god.
The flesh of Osiris Ani, triumphant, is the flesh of the Mighty One of terror.

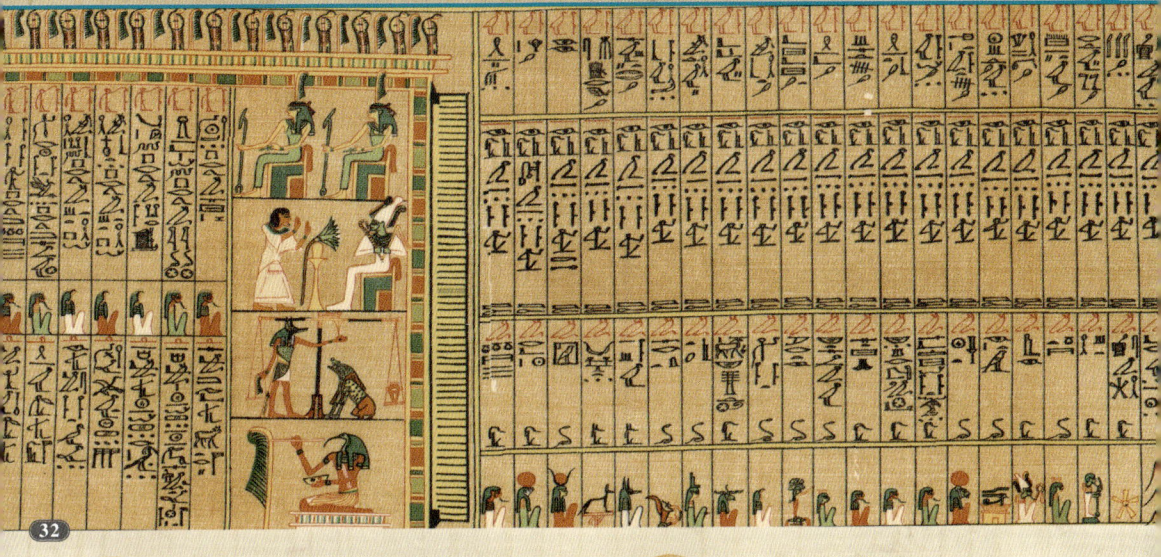

32

The goddess Sekhet, lion-headed, wearing a disk.
The reins and back of Osiris Ani, triumphant, are the reins and back of Sekhet.

An *utchat* upon a pylon.
The buttocks of Osiris Ani, triumphant, are the buttocks of the eye of Horus.

Osiris, wearing the *atef* crown and holding the flail and crook.
The privy member of Osiris Ani, triumphant, is the privy member of Osiris.

The goddess Nut.
The legs of Osiris Ani, triumphant, are the legs of Nut.

The god Ptah.
The feet of Osiris Ani, triumphant, are the feet of Ptah.

The star Orion.
The fingers of Osiris Ani, triumphant, are the fingers of Saah (Orion).

Three uraei.
The leg-bones of Osiris Ani, triumphant, are the leg-bones of the living uraei.

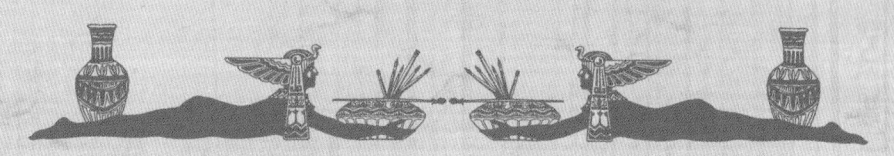

[THE NEGATIVE CONFESSION.]

Ani saith: 'Hail, thou whose strides are long, who comest forth from Annu, I have not done iniquity.'

'Hail, thou who art embraced by flame, who comest forth from Kheraba, I have not robbed with violence.'

'Hail, Fentiu, who comest forth from Khemennu, I have not stolen.'

'Hail, Devourer of the Shade, who comest forth from Qernet, I have done no murder; I have done no harm.'

'Hail, Nehau, who comest forth from Re-stau, I have not defrauded offerings.'

'Hail, god in the form of two lions, who comest forth from heaven, I have not minished [sic] oblations.'

'Hail, thou whose eyes are of fire, who comest forth from Saut, I have not plundered the god.'

'Hail, thou Flame, which comest and goest, I have spoken no lies.'

'Hail, Crusher of bones, who comest forth from Suten-henen, I have not snatched away food.'

'Hail, thou who shootest forth the Flame, who comest forth from Het-Ptah-ka, I have not caused pain.'

'Hail, Qerer, who comest forth from Amentet, I have not committed fornication.'

'Hail, thou whose face is turned back, who comest forth from thy hiding place, I have not caused shedding of tears.'

'Hail, Bast, who comest forth from the secret place, I have not dealt deceitfully.'

'Hail, thou whose legs are of fire, who comest forth out of the darkness, I have not transgressed.'

'Hail, Devourer of Blood, who comest forth from the block of slaughter, I have not acted guilefully.'

'Hail, Devourer of the inward parts, who comest forth from Mabet, I have not laid waste the ploughed land.'

'Hail, Lord of Right and Truth, who comest forth from the city of Right and Truth, I have not been an eavesdropper.'

'Hail, thou who dost stride backwards, who comest forth from the city of Bast, I have not set my lips in motion [against any man].'

'Hail, Sertiu, who comest forth from Annu, I have not been angry and wrathful except for a just cause.'

'Hail, thou, being of two-fold wickedness, who comest forth from Ati (?) I have not defiled the wife of any man.'

'Hail, thou two-headed serpent, who comest

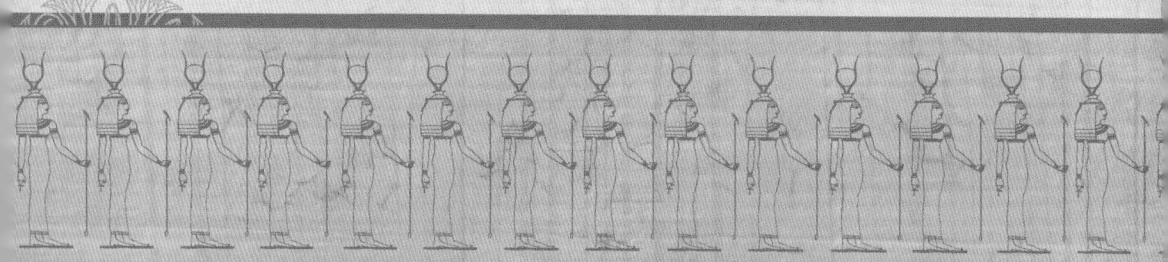

forth from the torture chamber, I have not defiled the wife of any man.'

'Hail, thou who dost regard what is brought unto thee, who comest forth from Pa-Amsu, I have not polluted myself.'

'Hail, thou Chief of the mighty, who comest forth from Amentet, I have not caused terror.'

'Hail, thou Destroyer, who comest forth from Kesiu, I have not transgressed.'

'Hail, thou who orderest speech, who comest forth from Urit, I have not burned with rage.'

'Hail, thou Babe, who comest forth from Uab, I have not stopped my ears against the words of Right and Truth.'

'Hail, Kenemti, who comest forth from Kenemet, I have not worked grief.'

'Hail, thou who bringest thy offering, I have not acted with insolence.'

'Hail, thou who orderest speech, who comest forth from Unaset, I have not stirred up strife.'

'Hail, Lord of faces, who comest forth from Netchfet, I have not judged hastily.'

'Hail, Sekheriu, who comest forth from Utten, I have not been an eavesdropper.'

Hail, Lord of the two horns, who comest forth from Saïs, I have not multiplied words exceedingly.'

'Hail, Nefer-Tmu, who comest forth from Het-Ptah-ka, I have done neither harm nor ill.'

'Hail, Tmu in thine hour, who comest forth from Tattu, I have never cursed the king.'

'Hail, thou who workest with thy will, who comest forth from Tebu, I have never fouled the water.'

'Hail, thou bearer of the sistrum, who comest forth from Nu, I have not spoken scornfully.'

Hail, thou who makest mankind to flourish, who comest forth from Saïs, I have never cursed God.'

'Hail, Neheb-ka, who comest forth from thy hiding place, I have not stolen.'

'Hail, Neheb-nefert, who comest forth from thy hiding place, I have not defrauded the offerings of the gods.'

'Hail, thou who dost set in order the head, who comest forth from thy shrine, I have not plundered the offerings to the blessed dead.'

'Hail, thou who bringest thy arm, who comest forth from the city of Maati, I have not filched the food of the infant, neither have I sinned against the god of my native town.'

'Hail, thou whose teeth are white, why comest forth from Ta-she, I have not slaughtered with evil intent the cattle of the god.'

PLATE 33

Alake of fire, at each corner of which is seated a dog-headed ape.

Rubric: Osiris Ani, triumphant, is girt about with [fine] raiment, he is shod with white sandals, and he is anointed with very precious anta ointment; and a bull, and herbs, and incense, and ducks, and flowers, and ale, and cakes have been offered unto him. And behold, thou shalt limn upon a clean tile the image of a table of offerings in clean colours, and thou shalt bury it in a field whereon swine have not trampled. If this word then be written upon it, he himself shall rise again, and his children's children shall flourish even as Ra flourisheth without ceasing. He shall dwell in favour in the presence of the king among the chiefs, and cakes and cups of drink and portions of meat shall be given unto him upon the table of the great god. He shall not be thrust from any door in Amentet; he shall travel on together with the kings of the North and of the South, and he shall abide with the followers of Osiris near unto Un-nefer, for ever, and for ever, and for ever.

A Tet.[104]

THE CHAPTER OF A TET OF GOLD: *Osiris Ani, triumphant, saith: 'Thou risest, O still heart! Thou shinest, O still heart! Place thou thyself upon my side. I have come and I have brought unto thee a tet of gold; rejoice thou in it.'*

A buckle, or tie.

THE CHAPTER OF A BUCKLE OF CARNELIAN: *Saith Osiris Ani, triumphant: 'The blood of Isis, the charms of Isis, the power of Isis, are a protection unto me, the chief, and they crush that which I abhor.'*

A heart.

THE CHAPTER OF A HEART OF CARNELIAN. *Saith Osiris Ani, triumphant: 'I am the* Bennu, *the soul of Ra, and the guide of the gods into the underworld. The souls come forth upon earth to do the will of their kas, and the soul of Osiris Ani cometh forth to do the will of his* ka.'

A headrest.

THE CHAPTER OF THE PILLOW WHICH IS PLACED UNDER THE HEAD OF OSIRIS ANI, TRIUMPHANT, TO WARD OFF WOES FROM THE DEAD BODY OF OSIRIS. *[Ani saith]: 'Lift up thy head to the heavens, for I have knit thee together triumphantly. Ptah hath overthrown his foes and thine; all his enemies have fallen, and they shall never more rise up again, O Osiris.'*

PLATE 33

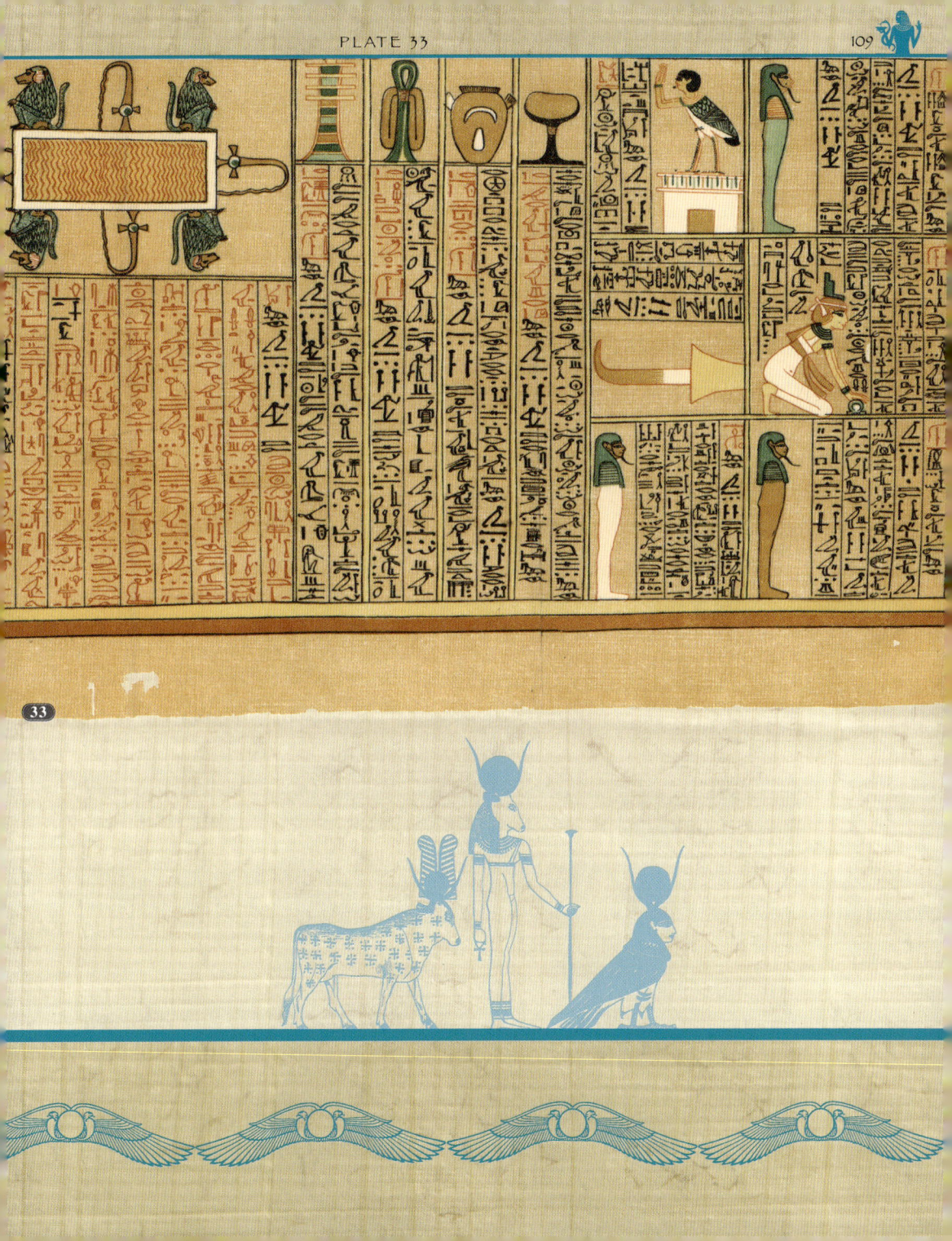

The mummy chamber, arranged as a plan, representing the floor and walls laid flat, in fifteen compartments. In the centre, under a canopy, is placed the bier bearing the mummy of Ani, beside which stands the god Anubis, with hands outstretched over the body. At the foot of the bier kneels the goddess Isis, and at the head the goddess Nephthys, each being accompanied by a flame of fire, which is placed in the compartment immediately behind her. The Tet occupies the compartment immediately above the bier, and the jackal emblematic of Anubis or Ap-uat lies on the tomb, while a sceptre with hanging *menats* occupies the compartment below. The four children of Horus, or gods of the cardinal points Mestha, Hapi, Tuamautef, and Qebhsennuf, stand in the corners of the four adjoining compartments. In each of the two upper and outer compartments is the human-headed bird emblematic of the soul, standing on a pylon. The one on the right is turned to the West or setting sun; the one on the left faces the East or rising sun. In the right lower compartment stands the figure of the Perfected Soul; in the corresponding compartment on the left is an Ushabti figure.

[Anubis, who dwelleth in the region of the embalmed, the chief of the holy house, layeth his hands upon the lord of life (i.e. the mummy), and provideth him with all that belongeth unto him, and saith: 'Hail to thee, thou beautiful one, the lord! Thou hast been gazed upon by the Sun's eye, thou hast been bound up by Ptah-Seker, thou hast been made whole by Anubis; breath hath been given unto thee by Shu, and thou hast been raised up by the fair one, the Prince of eternity. Thou hast thine eyes. Thy right eye is in the sektet boat, and thy left eye is in the atet boat. Thine eye-brows appear fair before the company of the gods. Thy brow is in the charge of Anubis. The back of thy head is in good case in the presence of the sacred hawk. Thy fingers are stablished by written decree in the presence of the lord of Khemennu, and Thoth giveth unto thee the speech of the sacred books. Thy hair is in good case in the presence of Ptah-Seker. Osiris is in bliss, and reverence is done unto him before the company of the great gods. He looketh upon the great god, he is led on fair paths, he is made strong with meals

of the tomb, and his enemies are cast down beneath him in presence of the company of the great gods who are in the great house of the aged one in Annu.'] [105]

[Isis saith:] 'I have come to be a protector unto thee. I waft unto thee air for thy nostrils, and the north wind, which cometh forth from the god Tmu, unto thy nose. I have made whole thy lungs. I have made thee to be like unto a god. Thine enemies have fallen beneath thy feet. Thou hast been made victorious in Nut, and thou art mighty to prevail with the gods.'

[Nephthys saith:] 'I have gone round about to protect thee, brother Osiris; I have come to be a protector unto thee. [My strength shall be behind thee, my strength shall be behind thee, for ever. Ra hath heard thy cry, and the gods have granted that thou shouldst be victorious. Thou art raised up, and thou art victorious over that which hath been done unto thee. Ptah hath thrown down thy foes, and thou art Horus, the son of Hathor.] ' [106]

[The flame of Isis saith:] 'I protect thee with this flame, and I drive away him (the foe) from the valley of the tomb, and I drive away the sand from thy feet. I embrace Osiris Ani, who is triumphant in peace and in right and truth.'

[The flame of Nephthys saith:] 'I have come to hew in pieces. I am not hewn in pieces, nor will I suffer thee to be hewn in pieces. I have come to do violence, but I will not let violence be done unto thee, for I am protecting thee.'

[The Tet saith:] 'I have come quickly, and I have driven back the footsteps of the god whose face is hidden. I have illumined his sanctuary. I stand behind the sacred Tet, or the day of repulsing disaster. I protect thee, O Osiris.'

[Mestha saith:] 'I am Mestha, thy son, O Osiris Ani, triumphant. I have come to protect thee, and I will make thine abode to flourish everlastingly. I have commanded Ptah, even as Ra himself commanded him.'

[Hapi saith:] 'I am Hapi thy son, O Osiris Ani, triumphant. I have come to protect thee. Thy head and thy limbs are knit together, and I have smitten down thine enemies beneath thee. I have given unto thee thy head for ever and for ever, O Osiris Ani, triumphant in peace.'

[Tuamautef saith:] 'I am thy beloved son Horus. I have come to avenge thee, O my father Osiris, upon him that did evil unto thee; and I have put him under thy feet for ever, and for ever, and for ever; O Osiris Ani, triumphant in peace.'

[Qebhsennuf saith:] 'I am thy son, O Osiris Ani, triumphant. I have come to protect thee. I have collected thy bones, and I have gathered together thy members. [I have brought thy heart and I have placed it upon its throne within thy body. I have made thy house to flourish after thee, O thou who livest for ever.]'

[The bird which faceth the setting sun saith]: 'Praise be to Ra when he setteth in the western part of heaven. Osiris Ani, triumphant in peace in the underworld, saith: "I am a perfected soul".'

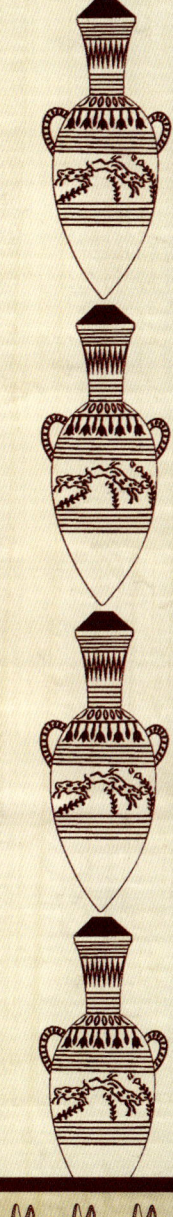

[The bird which faceth the rising sun saith]: 'Praise be to Ra when he riseth in the eastern part of heaven from Osiris Ani, triumphant.'

[The Perfected Soul saith]: 'I am a perfected soul in the holy egg of the abtu fish. I am the great cat which dwelleth in the seat of right and truth wherein riseth the god Shu.'

[The text near the Ushabti Figure reads]: Osiris Ani, the overseer, triumphant, saith: 'Hail, shabti figure! If it be decreed that Osiris [Ani] shall do any of the work which is to be done in the underworld, let all that standeth in the way be removed from before him; whether it be to plough the fields, or to fill the channels with water, or to carry sand from [the East to the West].' The shabti figure replies: 'I will do [it]; verily I am here [when] thou callest.'

Ani, with both hands raised in adoration, standing before a table of offerings; behind him is his wife holding lotus and other flowers in her left hand.

HERE BEGIN THE CHAPTERS OF THE SEKHET-HETEPU, AND THE CHAPTERS OF COMING FORTH BY DAY, AND OF GOING INTO AND OF COMING OUT FROM THE UNDERWORLD, AND OF ARRIVING IN THE SEKHET-AANRU, AND OF BEING IN PEACE IN THE GREAT CITY WHEREIN ARE FRESH BREEZES. Let me have power there. Let me become strong to plough there. Let me reap there. Let me eat there. Let me drink there. [Let me woo there.] And let me do all these things there, even as they are done upon earth.

Saith Osiris Ani, triumphant: 'Set hath carried away Horus to see what is being built in the Field of Peace, and he spreadeth the air over the divine soul within the egg in its day. He hath delivered the innermost part of the body of Horus from the holy ones of Akert (?). Behold I have sailed in the mighty boat on the Lake of Peace. I, even I, have crowned him in the House of Shu. His starry abode reneweth its youth, reneweth its youth. I have sailed on its Lake that I may come unto its cities, and I have drawn nigh unto the city Hetep. For behold, I repose at the seasons [of Horus]. I have passed through the region of the company of the gods who are aged and venerable. I have pacified the two holy Fighters[107] who keep ward upon life. I have done that which is right and fair, and I have brought an offering and have pacified the two holy Fighters. I have cut off the hairy scalp of their adversaries, and I have made aft end of the woes which befell [their] children; I have done away all the evil which came against their souls; I have gotten dominion over it, I have knowledge thereof. I have sailed forth on the waters [of the lake] that I may come unto the cities thereof. I have power over my mouth, being furnished [with] charms; let not [the fiends] get the mastery over me, let them not have dominion over me. May I be equipped in thy Fields of Peace. What thou wishest that shalt thou do, [saith the god].'

PLATE 35

The Sekhet-hetepet or 'Fields of Peace', surrounded and intersected with streams. They contain the following:

(a) Thoth, the scribe of the gods, holding pen and palette, introduces Ani, who is making an offering, and his *ka* to three gods who have the heads of a hare, serpent, and bull respectively, and are entitled *pauti*, 'the company of the gods'. Ani and a table of offerings in a boat. Ani addressing a hawk standing on a pylon-shaped pedestal, before which are an altar and a god. Three ovals. The legend reads: 'Being at peace in the Field [of Peace], and having air for the nostrils.'

(b) Ani reaping wheat, with the words 'Osiris reaps'; guiding the oxen treading out the corn; standing with hands raised in adoration behind the *bennu* bird, and holding the *kherp* sceptre, and kneeling before two vessels of red barley and wheat. The hieroglyphics seem to mean, 'the food of the shining ones'. Three ovals.

(c) Ani ploughing with oxen in a part of the Fields of Peace called 'Sekhet-aanre'; with the word *sekau*, to plough. The two lines of hieroglyphics read: 'Chapter of the River-horse. The river is one thousand [cubits] in its length. Not can be told its width. Not exist fishes any in it, not [exist] serpents any in it.'

(d) A boat bearing a flight of steps and floating on a stream. A boat of eight oars, each end shaped like a serpent's head, bearing a flight of steps; …at the bows [is written] *meter am Un-nefer*, 'the god therein is Un-nefer'. The stream that flows on the convex side of the small island is called *ashet pet*, 'flood (?) of [heaven]'. On the other island is placed a flight of steps. The space to the left represents the abode of the blessed dead, and is described as: 'The seat of the shining ones. Their length is cubits seven the wheat cubits three the blessed dead who are perfected they reap [it].'

PLATE 35   115

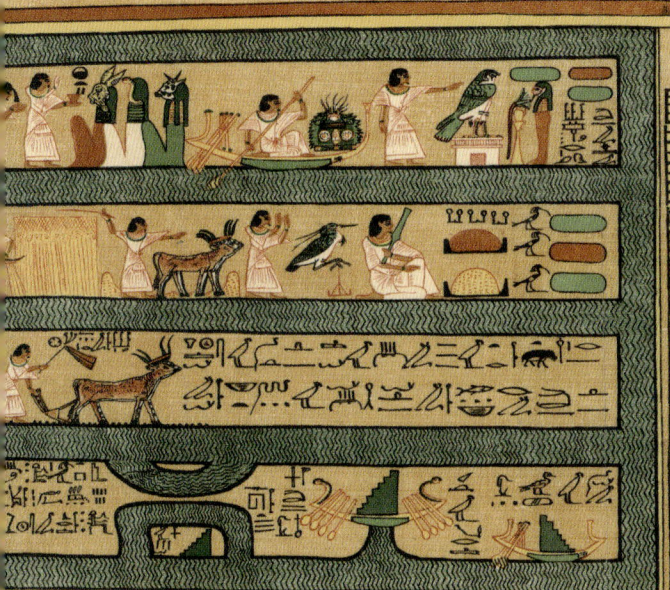

A hall, within which, on the left, Ani stands before two tables of offerings bearing libation water and lotus flowers, with hands raised, adoring Ra, hawk-headed (see page 115). Next are ranged seven cows, each one couchant before a table of offerings, and each having a *menat* attached to the neck;[108] and a bull standing before a table of offerings. Behind them are four rudders; and on the extreme right are four triads of gods, each triad having a table of offerings bearing a libation vase and a lotus flower (?).

36

Saith Osiris Ani, triumphant: 'Homage to thee, O thou lord, thou lord of right and truth, the One, the lord of eternity and creator of everlastingness, I have come unto thee, O my lord Ra. I have made meat offerings unto the seven kine and unto their bull. O ye who give cakes and ale to the shining ones, grant ye to my soul to be with you. May Osiris Ani, triumphant, be born upon your thighs; may he be like unto one of you for ever and for ever; and may he become a glorious being in the beautiful Amenta.'

[Address to the Rudders]: 'Hail, thou beautiful Power,[109] *thou beautiful rudder of the northern heaven.'*

'Hail, thou who goest round about heaven, thou pilot of the world, thou beautiful rudder of the western heaven.'

'Hail, thou shining one, who livest in the temple wherein are the gods in visible forms, thou beautiful rudder of the eastern heaven.'

'Hail, thou who dwellest in the temple of the bright-faced ones, thou beautiful rudder of the southern heaven.'

[Address to the four Triads]: 'Hail, ye gods who are above the earth, ye pilots of the underworld.'

'Hail, ye mother-gods who are above the earth, who are in the underworld, and who are in the House of Osiris.'

'Hail, ye gods, ye pilots of Tasert, ye who are above the earth, ye pilots of the underworld.'

'Hail, ye followers of Ra, who are in the train of Osiris.'

Ani standing before a table of offerings, with both hands raised in adoration. Behind him is his wife, wearing a lotus flower and a cone upon her head, and holding a sistrum and lotus flower in her left hand.

A HYMN OF PRAISE TO OSIRIS THE DWELLER IN AMENTET, UN-NEFER WITHIN ABTU, *Osiris Ani, triumphant, saith: 'Hail, O my lord, who dost traverse eternity, and whose existence endureth for ever. Hail, Lord of Lords, King of Kings, Prince, the God of*

gods who live with Thee, I have come unto Thee… Make thou for me a seat with those who are in the underworld, and who adore the images of thy ka and who are among those who [endure] for millions of millions of years…[110] *May no delay arise for me in Ta-mera. Grant thou that they all may come unto me, great as well as small. Mayest thou grant unto the ka of Osiris Ani [the power] to go into and to come forth from the underworld; and suffer him not to be driven back at the gates of the Tuat.'*

PLATE 37

A shrine wherein stands Seker-Osiris, lord of the hidden place, the great god, the lord of the underworld. He wears the white crown with feathers, and holds in his hands the sceptre, flail, and crook.

The goddess Hathor, in the form of a hippopotamus, wearing upon her head a disk and horns; in her right hand she holds an unidentified object, and in her left the emblem of life. Before her are tables of meat and drink offerings and flowers. Behind the hippopotamus, the divine cow, Meh-urit, symbolizing the same goddess, looks out from the funeral mountain, wearing the *menat* on her neck. At the foot of the mountain is the tomb, and in the foreground grows a group of flowering plants.

Hathor, lady of Amentet, dweller in the land of Urt, lady of Ta-sert, the Eye of Ra, the dweller in his brow, the beautiful Face in the Boat of Millions of Years…[111]

37

PLATE 37

ENDNOTES

1 The sistrum and *menat* were emblems of Thuthu's rank as a Chantress of Amun. (ed.)

2 Ra was the pre-eminent solar deity of the ancient Egyptians since the earliest times. He was later combined with the sun god Horus as Ra-Horakhty ('Ra, who is Horus of the Two Horizons'), and also with Amun, the 'king of the gods', as Amun-Ra. Usually Ra is depicted in human form, sometimes with the head of a falcon, sometimes without. (ed.)

3 The god Khepera is a phase of the night-sun, at the twelfth hour of the night, when he 'becomes' the rising sun.

4 The goddess Nut represented the sky, and perhaps also the exact place where the sun rose.

5 Manu is the name given to the mountains on the western bank of the Nile, opposite Thebes, wherein was situated the chief site of rock-hewn tombs.

6 Maat, 'daughter of the Sun, and queen of the gods', is the personification of righteousness, truth and justice.

7 'Horus of the two horizons' is the day-sun from his rising in the eastern horizon to his setting in the western horizon. The word *ka* means 'image' (and is often equated with the life-force). The deceased is always identified with Osiris, or the sun which has set. As the sun sets in the West and rises again in the East, so the dead man is laid in his tomb on the western bank of the Nile.

8 A name for the boat of the evening sun.

9 Thoth was the scribe of the gods and the personification of divine intelligence. His wife was the goddess Maat. (ed.)

10 The enemy of Ra was darkness and night, or any cloud that obscured the light of the sun.

11 The great temple of Ra at Heliopolis.

12 Apep, the serpent, personifies darkness, which Horus or the rising sun must conquer before he can reappear in the East.

13 The *abtu* and the *ant* fishes are sometimes depicted on coffins swimming at the bows of the boat of the sun.

14 A name of the boat of the rising sun.

15 Osiris, the night sun, was the son of Ra, and the father and son of Horus. He is always represented as a mummy holding in his hands the sceptre, crook and flail.

16 The site of the tombs on the western bank of the Nile.

17 Both Busiris [Tattu or Tettet] and Abydos [Abtu] claimed to be the resting place of the body of Osiris.

18 A name of Osiris when his scattered limbs had been brought together and built up again into a body by Isis and Nephthys. The name means 'lord of entirety'.

19 'The one who draws the world.'

20 Seker is a form of the night sun.

21 A name of Osiris.

22 Akert, Ta-sert, Neter-khert and Tuat (or Duat) are all names of the underworld, the realm of which Osiris was the prince. (ed.)

23 An or Ani, a name or form of Ra, the sun god.

24 A division of the 'Fields of Peace' (see Plate 35) or 'Field of Reeds', the paradisal realm wherein the souls of the blessed were supposed to reap and sow. (ed.)

25 Ammit has the hindquarters of a hippopotamus, the forelegs of a lion and the head of a crocodile. She devoured the dead whose hearts tipped the scales unfavourably. (ed.)

26 The four gods of the cardinal points, Mestha, Hapi, Tuamautef, and Qebhsennuf.

27 A class of divine beings.

28 This sentence appears to be unfinished.

29 Rearing cobras.

30 A priest of the god Ptah at Memphis. (ed.)

31 It is similar in shape to the chests that held the four jars containing the mummified intestines of the deceased.

32 This instrument is called *ur hekau*, and is made of a sinuous piece of wood, one end of which is in the form of a ram's head surmounted by an uraeus.

33 Mestha, Hapi, Tuamautef, Qebhsennuf, the gods of the cardinal points.

34 A name of the temple of Ra in Heliopolis.

35 The god of Tettetu [or Tattu], or Busiris, a town that was believed to contain the body of Osiris.

36 A name of Osiris.

37 'The door of the passages of the tomb.'

38 According to a text at Edfu, the neck of Osiris was preserved there.

39 'Casting up the earth' means the day of digging the grave.

40 The name of the chief priest of Ptah at Memphis.

41 The day of the festival of Seker was celebrated in the various sanctuaries of Egypt at dawn, 'the moment when the sun casts its golden rays upon the earth'. The *hennu* boat was drawn round the sanctuary.

42 Greek writers called this bird the phoenix, and the Egyptians considered it to be the soul of both the sun-god Ra and Osiris. (ed.)

43 The *utchat* or *wedjat* (the symbolic 'eye of Horus') was a protection against evil. (ed.).

44 'He dwelleth in his flame.'

45 'He who is in his hour.'

46 'Red of both eyes.'

47 'Flame seeing in the night.'

48 'Bringing by day.'

49 i.e. the sun god when he sets and rises.

50 Shu was the son of Ra and Hathor and the twin brother of Tefnut. He typified the sunlight, and separated the earth from the sky, which he established and supported.

51 i.e. 'substance of the gods'.

52 Or, 'I am he that presideth over the arrangement (or ordering) of things'.

53 This god was associated with Amun-Ra, and represented the power of reproduction.

54 i.e. 'the door of the passages of the tomb'.

55 i.e. the 'Pool of Double Truth'.

56 The eye of the Sun.

57 The Egyptian name for the constellation of the Great Bear.

58 i.e. 'He doth not give his flame, he dwelleth in the fire'.

59 i.e. 'He goeth in at his hour'.

60 i.e. 'He that hath two red eyes, the dweller in Het-Anes'. Het-Anes (i.e. the 'house of cloth') was a district belonging to the temple of Suten-henen or Heracleopolis in Upper Egypt.

61 i.e. 'Blazing-face coming forth, going back'.

62 i.e. 'The one who seeth by night, and leadeth by day'.

63 It appears that the scribe of the Ani papyrus has here accidentally omitted a section; the text is therefore supplied within brackets from the Nebseni papyrus.

64 Note the play upon the words *maau*, 'cat', and *maau*, 'like'.

65 Or instruments of death.

66 i.e. the 'Oppressor'.

67 The one with a knife.

68 i.e. Great Slayer.

69 House or mansion. In the upper line of Plates 11 and 12 there is a series of seven *Arits*, or mansions, through which the deceased is supposed to pass. In the lower line are the ten *Sebkhets*, or pylon-shaped gateways.

70 'Reversed of face: of many forms.'

71 'The voice that travelleth.'

72 i.e. the *Arit*.

73 i.e. 'Eater of his own filth'.

74 i.e. 'Making to lift up his face'.

75 i.e. 'Great One'.

76 i.e. Horus and Set.

77 i.e. 'Repulsing the face, great of speech'.

78 i.e. 'Repulser of the crocodile'.

79 i.e. 'He liveth upon worms'.

80 *Khakeru* or *khekeru* decorations represent the plants (usually reeds) used to top roofs. (ed.)

81 A broom made of twigs tied around a stick. (ed.)

82 i.e. 'Protecting his body'.

83 i.e. 'He maketh himself'.

84 This and its companion vignette and the vignettes of Plates 13–14 form one composition.

85 Osiris is also called An-maut-f.

86 i.e. the Fields of Peace.

87 The words are explained to mean, 'the daybreak on the sarcophagus of Osiris'.

88 This section, omitted in the Ani papyrus, is supplied from the papyrus of Nebseni.

89 Literally 'iron of heaven'.

90 i.e. the sky.

91 The judgment hall of Osiris, in which hearts were weighed.

92 The heavenly Memphis.

93 A class of divine beings.

94 The chapter as here given is incomplete; the missing words are: 'pleasant for us, pleasant is the hearing, and there is gladness of heart at the weighing of words. Let not lies be spoken against me near the god, in the presence of the great god, the lord of Amentet. Verily, how great shalt thou be when thou risest up in triumph!'

95 The text here appears to be corrupt, or at least some words have been omitted.

96 The text of the rest of this chapter is corrupt.

97 In other early papyri these two chapters form one; the division probably arose from a blunder on the part of the scribe.

98 Some words are omitted here.

99 The god Seker was a form of the night-sun, like Ptah, Osiris and Tanen.

100 The name of a constellation.

101 This chapter is generally entitled 'The Book of making perfect (or strong) the *khu* in the netherworld, in the presence of the great company of the gods'.

102 Or 'thou art exalted'.

103 The rubric to this chapter is found in another papyrus.

104 The Tet represents four pillars, i.e. the four quarters of heaven, or the whole universe. As a religious emblem it symbolizes the god Osiris.

105 The words spoken by Anubis are taken from a chapter in the Nebensi papyrus. (ed.)

106 In Ani the text is corrupt, and the passage within brackets is translated from the following version (Naville, *Todtenbuch*, Bd. II., Bl. 428):

107 Horus and Set.

108 In other papyri the names of these animals are given as follows: 'the dwelling of the *kas* of the lord of the universe'; 'orbit, the raising of the god'; 'the hidden one dwelling in her place'; 'the divine noble one of the North (?)'; 'the greatly beloved, red of hair'; 'the consort of life'; 'her name prevaileth in her dwelling'; 'Bull, making the kine to be fruitful'.

109 Variant 'his beautiful *ka*'.

110 The text of all this passage is corrupt, and the version here given is little more than a suggestion.

111 The few remaining words are corrupt.

GLOSSARY

abtu and ***ant*** fish – mythological fish that accompanied Ra, the sun-god, as he began his journey across the sky at sunrise in his celestial barque.

Abydos – according to tradition, the head of Osiris was buried here.

akh (or *khu*) – the *akh* was rendered a tangible reality by the reunion of the *ka* and the *ba* of the deceased.

Amenta – originally the place where the sun set, the name was subsequently applied to the cemeteries and tombs on the western bank of the Nile.

Ammit – part-crocodile, part-lion, part-hippopotamus, she was the 'devourer of the dead' and lived in Amenta, where she attended the ritual 'weighing of the heart'.

Amun (or Amen) – known as the 'king of the gods', Amun was the god of Thebes; the vast temple dedicated to him at Karnak lies on the west bank of the Nile, opposite Thebes (modern Luxor).

ankh – the Egyptian word for 'life'; its hieroglyph is a cross with a loop at the top.

Annu – one of the oldest cities and cult centres of ancient Egypt, often referred to by its Greek name of Heliopolis ('City of the Sun'). Annu is frequently mentioned in the Book of the Dead. According to Budge, the body of Osiris 'reposed in Annu' and the deceased made their way to Annu 'where souls were joined unto bodies…and the blessed dead lived on celestial food for ever'.

Anubis – the jackal-headed god who, having helped Isis embalm the body of Osiris after he had been killed and dismembered by Set, is associated with the mummification of the deceased. As protector of the deceased during the journey to the afterlife, he is depicted in several scenes in the Book of the Dead, including the rituals of the 'opening of the mouth' and the 'weighing of the heart'.

Apep – the enemy of Ra, the sun-god. Frequently depicted as a giant serpent, Apep represents darkness, clouds, or anything else that has the potential to obscure the sun on its daily journey across the sky. He was also said to battle against the sun-god at night, during the latter's eastward journey through the Duat or underworld.

ba – the soul or spirit, which enters each individual with the breath of life. When the physical body dies, the *ba* is able to move freely between the Netherworld and the world of the living. In the Book of the Dead it is depicted as a small bird with a human head.

bennu **bird** – said to be the soul of the sun-god Ra, having created itself from a fire burning in the temple of Ra. According to another myth, the *bennu* bird burst forth from the heart of Osiris.

crown – the triple or *atef* crown referred to in the Book of the Dead comprises a high central cone with a feather on each side. Worn by kings and gods alike, it is particularly associated with Osiris.

eye of Horus (also known as the *utchat* or *wedjat*) – Horus lost an eye during a fight with Set, but later regained it. Because his eye was retrieved, it became a symbol of healing and protection.

Geb – the earth-god, father of Isis, Osiris, Nephthys and Set.

Hathor – frequently depicted in the form of a cow with the solar disk between her horns, she was the goddess of love and beauty. In Thebes she was seen as a goddess of the dead and, as such, is depicted emerging from the mountain of Manu in the final vignette in the Book of the Dead of Ani.

Horus – son of Isis and Osiris; after Osiris had been killed by Set, Horus avenged his father by defeating Set and reclaiming his father's throne. (*See also* eye of Horus, Sons of Horus).

Isis – daughter of the sky-goddess Nut and the earth-god Geb; Isis was both sister and wife of Osiris, and the mother of his son Horus. Isis was the principal goddess of the Egyptian pantheon, revered as protector of both the living and the dead. Her cult extended beyond Egypt into the Graeco-Roman world.

ka – the life-force or spirit. Like the *ba*, the *ka* lived on after the death of the physical body, but it remained in the tomb with the mummy of the deceased and did not enjoy the freedom of movement of the *ba*.

Khepera – a form of the sun-god Ra. Khepera is frequently depicted as a scarab-headed figure because his rolling of the sun around its orbit echoed the way in which the scarab or dung beetle rolls a ball of dung containing its eggs, hiding it in a hole in the earth; when the eggs hatch, the newborn scarabs emerge from their hole. Khepera is particularly associated with the rising sun, which emerges from the earth anew each morning after its nightly passage through the underworld.

ma'at – the cosmic order, symbolized by the feather against which the deceased's heart is weighed in the judgement scene in the Book of the Dead. Maat is also personified as the goddess of harmony and justice; she wears an ostrich feather in her hair.

Manu – the name given to the western horizon and the region where the sun set.

Menat – a ceremonial object frequently associated with the goddess Hathor, comprising several strings of beads attached to a disc and a handle or counterpoise. It could be carried in the hand or worn as a necklace, in which case the counterpoise hung down the wearer's back. When shaken, the beads made a rattling sound to accompany song or dance.

Nephthys – daughter of sky-goddess Nut and the earth-god Geb, and sister to Isis, Osiris, and Set.

Nut – the sky-goddess, mother of Isis, Osiris, Nephthys, and Set.

opening of the mouth – a ceremonial ritual to restore the senses of the deceased, thereby enabling him or her to eat the offerings left in the tomb to sustain the *ka*. It also enabled the deceased to recite the appropriate utterances contained in the Book of the Dead and to address by name the various gods encountered on the journey through the underworld.

Osiris – son of the sky-goddess Nut and the earth-god Geb, Osiris was brother and husband of Isis, and father of Horus. As lord and ruler of the Duat or Netherworld, he is the protector and guide of the dead. He is frequently portrayed holding a crook and flail and wearing the *atef* crown, all three of which are symbols of kingship. He is sometimes depicted with green skin, a reminder that he was also a god of vegetation and fertility.

Ptah – a god with creative powers, who brought things into being by thinking of them in his mind and saying their name with his tongue. His name means 'Opener' and he is said to have devised the 'opening of the mouth' ritual.

Ra (or Re) – a sun-god. His victory over Apep preserves the cosmic order and ensures the continuity of life.

sceptre – some vignettes show Ani holding the *kherp* sceptre; originally a club or mace used in battle, the sceptre was a symbol of divine power.

Seb – an alternative name for the earth-god Geb.

Set (or Seth) – son of Nut and Geb, and the brother and murderer of Osiris.

Shu – Shu and his sister/wife Tefnut were the first gods created by Atum, the first of all gods. As the god of air, Shu is sometimes depicted holding up the canopy of the sky, thus separating it from the earth.

sistrum – a musical instrument comprising a handle surmounted by a looped frame containing rows of small metal disks which, when shaken, produced a jangling sound. It was used in many religious ceremonies, especially those associated with the goddess Hathor.

Sons of Horus – the gods Mestha, Hapi, Tuamautef, and Qebhsennuf were the gods of the four cardinal points (north, south, east and west). They also protected the internal organs of the deceased after their removal during the mummification process, which is why their heads ornament the lids of canopic jars (the containers in which the internal organs were preserved).

Tefnut – Tefnut and her brother/husband Shu were the first gods created by Atum, the first of all gods. As the goddess of moisture (or rain) and air, she is sometimes depicted helping Shu to hold up the canopy of the sky.

Thoth – the ibis-headed god of knowledge and wisdom. As the inventor of writing and scribe/record-keeper to the gods, Thoth is frequently depicted holding a scribe's palette and a pen (as in the 'weighing of the heart' scene in the Book of the Dead). He was also the messenger of the gods, which led to the Greeks identifying him with their god Hermes.

Tuat (or Duat) – the underworld, also known as Akert, Ta-sert, or Neter-khert.

uraeus – Greek name for the rearing cobra, the symbol of kingship, which adorns the foreheads or crowns of kings and gods.

utchat – See **eye of Horus**.